Wittgenstein and Theology

D1453514

Wittgenstein and Theology

Tim Labron

t&t clark

Published by T&T Clark
A Continuum imprint
The Tower Building   80 Maiden Lane
11 York Road   Suite 704
London SE1 7NX   New York, NY 10038

www.continuumbooks.com

British Library Cataloguing-in-Publication Data
A catalogue record for this book is available from the British Library

ISBN-10: HB: 0-567-17508-1
           PB: 0-567-60105-6
ISBN-13: HB: 978-0-567-17508-3
           PB: 978-0-567-60105-6

Typeset by Newgen Imaging Systems Pvt Ltd, Chennai, India
Printed on acid-free paper in Great Britain by MPG Books Ltd, Bodmin, Cornwall

Contents

Part I
Wittgenstein

Chapter 1
Introduction

Wittgenstein is arguably one of the most influential and important philosophers of the twentieth century. His influence covers a diverse spectrum of disciplines; including, philosophy of mind, language, mathematics, religion, logic, and epistemology. However, theology is not yet one of the prominent disciplines that Wittgenstein has influenced. One reason that he has not made a significant impact on theology is that his philosophy can be difficult to grasp and he does not offer a sustained discussion of theology. Moreover, it is difficult to ascertain what his particular beliefs are. Wittgenstein says, 'I am not a religious man but I cannot help seeing every problem from a religious point of view.'[1] This state of not being religious, but having a religious point of view, leads to many different conclusions. For example, we may ask the following questions: 'Does Wittgenstein's philosophy lead to atheism?', 'Is it clearly religious?' Perplexingly, both of these questions have been answered in the affirmative. For instance, Brian Clack[2] agrees with the former and Phillip Shields[3] with the latter. Compounding the lack of consensus is the problem of associating Wittgenstein's philosophy with the so-called Wittgensteinian Fideism. This problematic label was coined and generated by the atheist philosopher Kai Nelson – not Wittgenstein or Wittgensteinians. Wittgenstein's philosophy has found good use amongst some post-liberal theologians to advance their studies in language, context and meaning. However, the use of Wittgenstein by some of these theologians is often less about Wittgenstein's philosophy as it stands and more about extracting aspects of his thought as utilities to fit their own positions.

It is therefore difficult to understand Wittgenstein's philosophy through the lens of theology and the philosophy of religion in light of the multitude of voices and contradictions. Why study his philosophy if it is simply atheistic, can be reduced to fideism, or reduces meaning to mere language-games? Alternatively, why study Wittgenstein's philosophy if it is not substantial on its own, and is at best only a tool to bolster various theological points of view, such as post-liberalism? My answer is that we need to discuss Wittgenstein precisely because of these types of questions – they all show that there is a need to let Wittgenstein's philosophy address theology on its own.

In order to understand and apply Wittgenstein's philosophy to theology it is necessary to discuss it as it stands, and then apply it to theology. Yet this is not a simple task. The difficulty, however, does not reside in intellectual capacity. Rather, as Wittgenstein says,

> What makes a subject hard to understand – if it's something significant and important – is not that before you can understand it you need to be specially trained in abstruse matters, but the contrast between understanding the subject and what most people want to see. Because of this the very things which are most obvious may become the hardest of all to understand. What has to be overcome is a difficulty having to do with the will, rather than with the intellect.[4]

Wittgenstein's philosophy is unique and does not fit the traditional setting of competing theories and explanations. He does not offer another theory that we could discuss on its own; rather, he rejects theories. Since he rejects rather than creates theories, does that mean that his philosophy is nihilistic? The answer is no, and we should instead see his philosophy in an affirmative light since it can usefully clarify philosophical problems. In a sense, his philosophy is more like a virus checker on your computer that removes theories, in contrast to adding another theory. Wittgenstein writes,

> where does our investigation get its importance from, since it seems to only destroy everything interesting, that is, all that is great and important? (As it were all the buildings, leaving behind only bits of stone and rubble.)

What we are destroying is nothing but houses of cards
and we are clearing up the ground of language on which
they stand.[5]

The question then becomes, 'Do we have the *will* to let Wittgenstein
remove the theory, or do we prefer to continually replace one
theory with another theory?'

To show this unique nature of his philosophy it is productive
to discuss it in action and show how it contrasts with and works
against the prevalent tradition, that is, to show how it cleans
what he regards to be theories. Once again, it is important to
note that Wittgenstein is not replacing one theory with another;
he removes them. This then leaves the host to function properly.
It is therefore necessary to spend some time discussing the philosophical tradition and malware that he works with in order to
see his philosophy in relief. Indeed, the *via negativa* of theology is
a helpful tool to discuss Wittgenstein's philosophy.

In particular, the following discussion will focus on the
problematic tradition of separating humans from the world, or
in other words, separating ideas from the external world, and
separating God from the human context. Wittgenstein regards
this separation to be in a close affinity with scepticism since the
separation created by philosophical theories makes it difficult
to then grasp the distant world and God. In a sense, this will
be the virus that he removes in philosophy and, since this same
virus infects theology, his useful approach in philosophy can be
applied analogically to theology.

For example, Descartes, who is known as the father of modern philosophy (and whom Wittgenstein critiques indirectly
throughout the *Philosophical Investigations*), questions the relationship between ideas and the external world. Once this separation
is opened, it leaves room for the sceptic's questions – 'Is the link
between my mind and the external world accurate?' Descartes
takes the sceptic's questions to heart and ends with the mainstay
of his method; namely, to move away from the uncertain world
to his own thinking (rationalism). Subsequent philosophers have
taken Descartes' lead and have tried alternative answers to the
sceptic's concerns. For example, Locke tries to connect the individual's perceptions with the external world in terms of qualities

and with the probability that the material world generates our ideas (empiricism and realism), but he ends with the external world being an unknown something. Berkeley, on the other hand, sees the logical conclusion of Locke's project and runs with it by concluding that all we have are ideas so the world is immaterial and created by ideas (idealism).

Descartes and Locke maintain the separation between ideas and the world while Berkeley collapses the physical world into ideas. In each case the human aspect of daily life is devalued in terms of knowledge, or at least set aside in favour of theories and abstractions. Wittgenstein rejects these theories and explanations, but he does not offer a better theory or explanation to refute the sceptic. Instead, he goes back to the original problem of separating meaning and knowledge from the world and rejects it as a starting point. Wittgenstein does not intend to mend the gap the virus created; he deletes the virus that created it.

This may appear to be a long route to discuss Wittgenstein's philosophy, but it is perhaps the best exemplification of his thought and as Wittgenstein says in his *Remarks on Frazer*, 'To convince someone of what is true, it is not enough to state it; we must find the road from error to truth.'[6] Moreover, he observes, 'In philosophy the winner of the race is the one who can run most slowly. Or: the one who gets there last.'[7] Indeed, the route to show the nature of Wittgenstein's philosophy follows his analogy: 'What is your aim in philosophy? – To show the fly the way out of the fly-bottle.'[8] That is, to retrace the confused notions that have caught philosophy and to head backwards to their source, just as the fly needs to retrace its steps backwards to get out of the bottle; rather than devise more ways of continually bumping against the sides.

Descartes, Locke and Berkeley are chosen not only to show what Wittgenstein views as the problematic tradition of separation and scepticism in philosophy, but also to show the analogical arguments and problems found in theology; namely, Platonism, Nestorianism, and Eutychianism respectively. Once again, the philosophical question will centre on the relationship between ideas and the world, while the theological question will centre on the relationship between the divine and the human. Moreover, as Wittgenstein's philosophy helpfully addresses the philosophical problems, the Council of Chalcedon similarly addresses theological (Christological) problems on an analogical basis. This useful parallel between the corrective nature of both the Council of Chalcedon and Wittgenstein's philosophy, in their respective domains, provides the most effective example by which his philosophy can meaningfully enter theological discourse. I will argue that Wittgenstein's philosophy and the Council of Chalcedon join what realism and Nestorianism think are radically separate, and make distinct what idealism and Eutychianism think is a radical unity. The philosopher who grasps Wittgenstein's philosophy should be able to see the significance of Chalcedon, and the theologian who understands Chalcedon, should be able to grasp the significance of Wittgenstein's philosophy.

To compare Wittgenstein's philosophy with theology is a useful endeavour, even though it would be completely wrong-headed to make such a comparison on the grounds that he is a Christian or even religious. On the other hand, it would not be accurate to say that Wittgenstein was an atheist. What is clear is that he never rejects religion nor does he clearly endorse it. Nonetheless, Wittgenstein had read the Bible[9] and once told M. O'C. Drury: 'There is a sense in which you and I are both Christians.'[10] What did this mean? Rather than arguing about matters in Wittgenstein's personal life, I will approach these questions in terms of his philosophy and relate them analogically to theology. His remark is interesting on this point: 'When I think of the Jewish Bible, the Old Testament on its own, I feel like saying: the head is (still) missing from this body. These problems have not been solved. These hopes have not been fulfilled.'[11] I suggest that these remarks, from the standpoint of a theological discussion, can help to clarify the nature of Wittgenstein's early thought as compared to his later thought and will thereby show how his later thought in particular is analogical with Chalcedonian Christology.

For example, much debate has centred on the relationship between the early and later Wittgenstein. Is there a radical break, or is there a clear continuity with little difference between the early and later Wittgenstein? His remark regarding the Old and New Testaments, along with a discussion of his thought, can help to make this relationship clear. For instance, the Old Testament and the New Testament represent continuity but are different; likewise, Wittgenstein's early thought and later thought also represent continuity but are different. Indeed, the New Testament can only be understood comprehensively by understanding the Old Testament, and Wittgenstein says, 'It suddenly seemed to me that I should publish those old thoughts and the new ones together: that the latter could be seen in the right light only by contrast with and against the background of my old way of thinking.'[12] The analogy between Wittgenstein's philosophy and theology is based on the early Wittgenstein separating an underlying logical syntax from the human use of language and the Old Testament separation of God from human flesh. While the later Wittgenstein shifts his understanding of logic from being hidden to being shown *in* our use of language, and the New Testament shows God *in* the flesh. The separation of God from the world and logic from the world is eased in both Wittgenstein's later thought and Christian theology – both of which can be viewed from a Christian perspective as emphasising the shown and the revealed respectively.

Wittgenstein's philosophy can also be helpfully compared to what Luther calls the 'theology of the cross'. Both reject rationalism and the assumed human ability to climb ladders from the human condition to metaphysical knowledge. Both regard such a ladder as an erroneous device that ends with metaphysical confusion. In such cases Wittgenstein notes, 'We have got on to slippery ice where there is no friction and so in a certain sense the conditions are ideal, but also, just because of that, we are unable to walk. We want to walk: so we need *friction*. Back to the rough ground!'[13] We know logic as shown in our use of words and we know God as shown in the Word made flesh. Indeed, the language of the earliest church is not that of philosophers speculating on truth in the abstract, it is the language of tax collectors, farmers and fishers.

What Wittgenstein shows in philosophy can apply to theology; namely, our reality and meaning are social and language based, and set in a tradition and history – it is human. Attention must be given to words at work in philosophy and the Word in the flesh in theology. Therefore, the task of the philosopher and theologian is not to provide theories of meaning, but is to show meaning in words and practices. When we turn to concrete examples there is no theory required since the words are no longer deprived of their meaning. What combats the separation between God and humans, ideas and the world and the resultant scepticism, is not apologetic theories, but redemption – as Wittgenstein says, 'What combats doubt is, as it were, *redemption*. Holding fast to this must be holding fast to belief.'[14]

Chapter 2

Short Biography

Wittgenstein was a unique philosopher who did not fit the stereotypical Cambridge professor of philosophy. He clearly was a cultured man with fine tastes in such things as music and architecture, but at the same time, he was very down to earth. He had complained on occasion to the host of a lavish meal that had been prepared for him since a boiled egg would suffice. He enjoyed 'silly' American movies over English and Continental movies since he regarded the latter as pompous. Wittgenstein himself notes, 'A typical American film, naïve and silly, can – for all its silliness and even *by means of* it – be instructive. A fatuous, self-conscious English film can teach one nothing. I have often learnt a lesson from a silly American film.'[15] In particular, he enjoyed the 'dancing of Ginger Rogers and Fred Astaire'.[16] Wittgenstein also had a certain preference for what may be considered silly literature over serious literature. He often used examples from *Detective Story Magazine* – which he read frequently including during the last days of his life – rather than esteemed philosophical journals or classic philosophical works for his discussions. Moreover, he remarked, 'as little philosophy as I have read I have certainly not read too little, *rather too much*. I see that whenever I read a philosophical book: it doesn't improve my thoughts at all, it makes them worse.'[17]

He would often recommend to his students that they do something useful like work in a department store instead of continuing in philosophy; indeed, he continually had the urge to leave academia himself since he regarded his academic life as one that would slowly lead to his death. It may be a stretch, but the pride he is reported to have had in the high temperature of his baths likely outweighed any pride he may have had in his post as a Professor of Philosophy. Indeed, Wittgenstein once remarked 'A philosopher should enjoy no more prestige than a plumber!'[18]

Ludwig Wittgenstein was born in Vienna on 26 April 1889; the eighth and last child. His mother was Catholic and he was baptized as a Catholic. His father's side was of Jewish descent, but his grandfather converted to Protestantism. The Wittgensteins were a wealthy and culturally astute family; indeed, Johannes Brahms was a friend of the family and Ravel composed *Piano Concerto for the Left Hand* for his brother Paul after he lost his right arm during the war. Wittgenstein himself played the clarinet (and was reported to be an amazing whistler) which he carried in a sock rather than a case.

After completing his matriculation he was interested in studying Physics with Ludwig Boltzmann; however, in 1906 Boltzmann's suicide put that idea to rest and he turned to mechanical engineering in Berlin but found it to be very unsatisfactory. In 1908 he then went to Manchester England to study engineering at Manchester University. He began to research an aero-engine that did not use pistons. However, it was the development of the propeller profile in particular that eventually caught Wittgenstein's attention and developed into mathematical questions and then importantly into questions regarding the foundations of mathematics. This interest in mathematical foundations led him to read Bertrand Russell's work *The Principles of Mathematics*. It was Russell's work along with Frege's *Grundgesetze der Arithmetik* that initiated Wittgenstein's entry into philosophy. In short: the issue at hand was to prove that logic and mathematics are both objective studies, and that mathematics can be shown to have a logical foundation; however, the proof for the logical foundation of mathematics remained elusive. Russell wrote: 'What the complete solution of the difficulty may be, I have not succeeded in discovering; but as it affects the very foundations of reasoning, I earnestly commend the study of it to the attention of all students of logic.'[19] For Wittgenstein the engineering became less important and he was caught by Russell's questions and challenge.

In the autumn of 1911 Wittgenstein went to Cambridge to talk with Russell in person and to work out whether he should continue in aeronautics or begin to study philosophy in earnest. Russell told Wittgenstein to write an essay and apparently the first sentence convinced Russell that Wittgenstein should study philosophy. Russell, despite the eventual disagreement between the two, later noted that 'Getting to know Wittgenstein was one of the most exciting intellectual adventures of my life.'[20]

Wittgenstein moved into Trinity College on 1 February 1912, but not without a challenge. His search for furniture was apparently exasperating; he continually rejected the furniture he was shown because of the excessive ornamentation that was not essential to the construction. His perspective on furniture even applied to a friend's search, to whom he remarked, 'do you wish to take the one which the furniture manufactures submitted? If so do insist that they cut off all those measly fancy ends. And why should the bed stand on rollers? You're not going to travel about with it in your house!?'[21]

Wittgenstein's father died in January 1913 leaving Wittgenstein a substantial inheritance that was put to use, in part, to support artists without means. Shortly thereafter Wittgenstein became disillusioned with what he considered to be the shallow and overly intellectual Cambridge atmosphere, so he moved to Skjolden, Norway to continue his questions in logic. Some notes from this early period have been preserved and, in particular, the earliest is TS 201 with the title *Notes on Logic* with notes by Russell. This manuscript is held at the Russell Archive of McMaster University in Ontario, Canada.

As the First World War approached in 1914, Wittgenstein retuned to Vienna and sought enlistment even though he was excused from duty due to a hernia. Apparently, the notion to enlist was not purely patriotic according to his sister Hermine, who noted that he sought a demanding alternative to intellectual work. Wittgenstein himself notes, 'Perhaps the nearness of death will bring light into my life. God enlighten me.'[22] Between 1914 and 1918 Wittgenstein served active duty and he continued to complete his work on the manuscripts which he kept in his backpack, including those that would become the *Tractatus Logico-Philosophicus*. That Wittgenstein was able to continue his thoughts on logic is not because he had a simple administrative posting. Rather, it was in spite of the fact that he was placed with an artillery regiment on the Galician front, and it was there that he worked on MS 103 published in *Notebooks, 1914–1916*. Although he was working on questions in logic, his primary reading was not logic. Arriving in Galicia Wittgenstein purchased the only book he could find in the bookshop – Tolstoy's *Gospel in Brief*, which he completely digested and carried with him everywhere. In 1916 Wittgenstein was sent to the Russian front and one of the items he took with him was Dostoevsky's *The Brothers Karamazov* of which he memorized large portions.

Wittgenstein was decorated several times for his duty and was recommended for the Gold Medal of Valour, but was given the Band of the Military Service Medal with Swords for his bravery. By 1918 Wittgenstein, in spite of his active service, completed the *Tractatus Logico-Philosophicus*. That November he was taken prisoner by the Italians. He commented about this time as a prisoner to Drury, who reflected upon the long and significant history of liturgical prayers.

> Yes, those prayers read as if they had been soaked in
> centuries of worship. When I was a prisoner of war in
> Italy we were compelled to attend mass on Sundays.
> I was very glad of that compulsion . . . But remember
> the Christian religion does not consist in saying a lot of
> prayers, in fact we are commanded just the opposite. If
> you and I are to live religious lives it must not be that we
> talk a lot about religion, but that in some ways our lives
> are different.[23]

During this time he was considering abandoning philosophy and becoming a primary school teacher since he thought he had completed his philosophical task.

When Wittgenstein was released from captivity, he returned to Vienna and immediately gave away the rest of his inheritance. Unsurprisingly, his notary remarked, 'you want to commit financial suicide!'[24] Academically Wittgenstein was also on the edge as his attempts to have the *Tractatus* published proved to be futile, as was the attempt by Russell and Frege to understand it. Wittgenstein eventually gave up and sent the text to Russell to sort out. He then moved to a monastery near Vienna to work as a gardener until he finally took a post as a primary school teacher in September 1921 – the year that the *Tractatus* was finally published by C. K. Ogden (editor) and Kegan Paul (publisher). Subsequent to the publication of the *Tractatus* inquiries were being made into the possibility of Wittgenstein working towards a Ph.D. as his work was beginning to be discussed, particularly through a discussion group centred on Moritz Schlick and which was to become the Vienna Circle – they considered Wittgenstein's ideas to be very significant and to require further discussion.

By 1926 Wittgenstein's primary school teaching days were numbered (he taught from 1921–1926) for several reasons. He was not entirely happy with the post and the villagers were rather suspicious of his general demeanour and his strict teaching style – but they were elated that he fixed the local factory's steam engine when no one else could! By April 1926, he was released from his primary school teaching duties and he once again became a gardener in a monastery – shortly thereafter his mother died.

Wittgenstein showed further dexterity as he subsequently worked on the design of his sister's house until 1928 including minute details for the windows, doors, and radiators. His attention to detail – including importing parts since local companies could not produce them to his exacting standard – was exasperating to his fellow workers. Overall, and perhaps unsurprisingly, the house did not have excessive ornamentation, not because there were insufficient funds; rather, that was his style. Indeed, rather than chandeliers he had bare bulbs installed. He still kept up his philosophy intermittently through occasional meetings with members of the Schlick group, but it was not until 1929 that he met with Schlick in Vienna, and this is recorded in *Wittgenstein and the Vienna Circle*.

It was in 1929 when Wittgenstein decided he could return to philosophy and Cambridge. His *Tractatus Logico-Philosophicus* was accepted as his doctoral work and he was granted a fellowship and position as Research Fellow for 5 years back at Trinity College. He began to shift his philosophical perspective by this point and was becoming less concerned with determining the underlying logical syntax of language. In 1930 he met his friend Druy in a distressed mood, and then tellingly remarks:

> I was walking about in Cambridge and passed a
> bookshop, and in the window were portraits of Russell,
> Freud and Einstein. A little further on, in a music shop,
> I saw portraits of Beethoven, Schubert and Chopin.
> Comparing these portraits I felt intensely the terrible
> degeneration that had come over the human spirit in the
> course of only a hundred years.[25]

Wittgenstein's thought began to take a new turn towards living culture in contrast to mechanical deadness, and he began to continually insist that he was not developing theories, but was looking towards showing why we do not need theories. The new tack took the form of the *Blue Book* that was to substitute for lectures, and the *Brown Book* that further shows Wittgenstein formulating his thoughts. These works introduced the notion of the language-games and were the forerunners of the well-known *Philosophical Investigations*.

As the end of Wittgenstein's Research Fellowship at Trinity approached he considered taking a post in the Soviet Union. He made contacts through a friend with the Russian Ambassador in London – the meeting was one of the rare occasions that Wittgenstein wore a tie – and he studied Russian. Eventually he travelled to Leningrad and the Northern Institute, Moscow, and Kazakhstan where he was offered a chair at the University where Tolstoy had studied. Despite his links with Soviet academic institutions, what he really wanted was a manual labour job, but this clearly was not what the Soviet Union required at the time. Wittgenstein quickly decided against living in the Soviet Union. Monk notes that Wittgenstein thought it would be difficult 'for "people of our upbringing" to live there because of the degree of petty dishonesty that was necessary even to survive.' Moreover, he thought that 'living in Russia was rather like being a private in the army.'[26] The point here should not be read as Wittgenstein's feeling of superiority, he found the Cambridge life to be terribly superficial and artificial while he longed for the simple life of labour in the Soviet Union; instead, this should be read as his suspicion of and dislike of regimented and perhaps confused thinking, the very sort of thinking he disliked in philosophy. Wittgenstein even considered studying medicine and working with Dury in a psychiatric practice in Ireland to avoid professional philosophy.

In September 1935 Wittgenstein nonetheless turned back to philosophy, which was fostered by his latest favourite student Rush Rhees who became one of Wittgenstein's closest friends right to his death, one of his literary executors, and taught at the University of Wales, Swansea. Subsequently, Wittgenstein once again travelled to Norway to immerse himself in his work, and he was very productive in writing about one quarter of what was to become published as *Philosophical Investigations*.

The year 1938 brought immense change for Wittgenstein, not the least of which was the convergence of Austria with Nazi-Germany. Given this situation, and through advice from his friend Sraffa in particular, Wittgenstein considered changing his nationality and he applied for a position at Cambridge. Moore was retiring and becoming *emeriti* so Wittgenstein applied for the upcoming chair and was awarded it in 1939 along with his British citizenship. He was somewhat surprised that he received the academic post given that Professor Broad, who was a fellow of Trinity College and did not like Wittgenstein, wrote a reference. However, his reference noted, 'To refuse the chair to Wittgenstein would be like refusing Einstein a chair of Physics.'[27] After his academic post and British citizenship were secure Wittgenstein strove, in light of his family's obvious difficulties with Jewish associations, to have the ancestral records of his family declare that their common grandfather, Hermann Christian Wittgenstein, was an ancestor of German blood – not without substantial payment to the Reich Office for research into Ancestry.

In August 1939, Wittgenstein returned to Cambridge, took up his post, and once again moved into his previous room in Whewells Court. However, during the war he was not satisfied with simply being an academic and an observer of the war. He thereby volunteered at Guy's Hospital in London and subsequently received great praise from the physician

R. T. Grant – whose research group was transferred, along with Wittgenstein, to Newcastle – who notes: 'he has a keen critical mind and in discussions of medical and physiological problems has proved a most helpful and stimulating colleague. He has undertaken observations on respiratory variations of blood pressure in man, devising his own experiments and apparatus. The results of his work so far are at variance with commonly accepted views and of considerable interest.'[28]

After his noteworthy medical research duties were completed in Newcastle he was unhappily on route to take up his post at Cambridge again. Fortunately, for Wittgenstein, he was granted a leave of absence from Cambridge to travel to Swansea, Wales to continue his work. Wittgenstein found Swansea to be much more satisfactory than Cambridge. He notes, 'I know quite a number of people here whom I like. I seem to find it more easy to get along with them here than in England. I feel much more often like smiling, e.g. when I walk the street, or when I see children, etc.'[29] His philosophical endeavours focused on publishing his new book, *Philosophical Investigations*, rather than his Cambridge Chair duties.

By the autumn of 1944, Wittgenstein had to return to Cambridge, even though his book was not finished and he was still unhappy with his academic position: 'Everything about the place repels me. The stiffness, the artificiality, the self-satisfaction of the people. The university atmosphere nauseates me.'[30] Iris Murdoch, who sat in on Wittgenstein's lectures comments:

> His extraordinary directness of approach and the
> absence of any sort of paraphernalia were the things that
> unnerved people . . . with most people, you meet them
> in a framework, and there are certain conventions about
> how you talk to them and so on. There isn't a naked
> confrontation of personalities. But Wittgenstein always
> imposed this confrontation on all his relationships.[31]

This indeed made his Cambridge life difficult, including his disagreements with Russell, who thought Wittgenstein had given up serious philosophy. By the end of 1947, Wittgenstein was no longer tied to his lectures or Cambridge.

In 1948 Wittgenstein spends more time in Ireland and by 1949 the collection of remarks that become the *Philosophical Investigations* are complete. Wittgenstein, however, noted: 'It will fall into hands which are not for the most part those in which I like to imagine it. May it soon – this is what I wish for it – be completely forgotten by the philosophical journalists, and so be preserved for a better sort of reader.'[32] This work was published *posthumously*.

In 1949, Wittgenstein travels to Ithaca, New York to visit his friend and former student Norman Malcolm, who took Wittgenstein to a philosophy meeting at Cornell University and the reaction of those gathered is revealing. John Nelson notes:

> Malcolm appeared approaching down the corridor. On his arm leaned a slight, older man, dressed in wind jacket and old army trousers. If it had not been for his face, alight with intelligence, one might have taken him for some vagabond Malcolm had found along the road and decided to bring him out of the cold. . . . Black, who was conducting this particular meeting, stood up and turned to his right and it became clear, to everyone's surprise . . . that he was about to address the shabby older man Malcolm had brought to the meeting. Then came the startling words; said Black, 'I wonder if you would be so kind, Professor Wittgenstein . . .' Well, when Black said 'Wittgenstein' a loud and instantaneous gasp went up from the assembled students. You must remember: 'Wittgenstein' was a mysterious and awesome name in the philosophical world of 1949, at Cornell in particular. The gasp that went up was just the gasp that would have gone up if Black has said 'I wonder if you would be so kind, Plato. . . .'[33]

Unfortunately, during his stay in New York Wittgenstein became ill and upon his return to England he was diagnosed with prostate cancer.

Wittgenstein spent the remaining two years of his life living with his friends and working on what is now published as *Remarks on Colours* and *On Certainty*. While staying with von

Wright, Wittgenstein was offered the chance to deliver the John Locke Lecture for 1950 at Oxford university, the financial gain would help him, and he was told that he had the chance to speak to more than 200 students and that there would be no discussion during the lecture – if you grasp the nature of Wittgenstein's teaching style, it is easy to understand why he rejected this offer. His lectures were not a matter of dictating notes to students; instead, his lectures were thought in live action and sometimes he would not allow notes to be taken. He then stayed with Elizabeth Anscombe in Oxford, where he asked to speak to a non-philosophical priest and was met by Father Conrad, a Dominican priest who was influential in the conversion of Wittgenstein's friends Yorick and Anscombe herself. He thought of planning a trip to Norway, or to stay in a Monastery again, but his health dictated that he make continual trips to the hospital in Cambridge. Eventually, due to his failing health, he moved into his Physician's home since he did not want to die in a hospital. When his treatments stopped and he knew that he had only a couple months to live he completed over half of *On Certainty*. When told he had a couple of days to live and that his friends were arriving he said, 'Tell them I've had a wonderful life.' That night of 28 April 1951, he lost consciousness.

When Ben, Anscombe, Smythies and Drury arrived, Smythies had also invited Father Conrad. The friends debated whether or not Father Conrad should proceed with prayers and rituals and the usual rites for the dying. It is clear that they did not regard Wittgenstein as obviously opposed to Christianity, but not exactly a Christian either. Eventually they decided to proceed since, as Drury remembered, Wittgenstein hoped that his friends prayed for him. In 1944, Wittgenstein remarked, 'I seem to be surrounded now by Roman Catholic converts! I don't know whether they pray for me. I hope they do.'[34] Wittgenstein died that morning and was given a Catholic burial at St Giles Church, Cambridge.

How should we understand Wittgenstein's life and work? It is worthwhile to end with his remark to Drury: 'Bach wrote on the title page of his *Orgelbüchlein*, "To the glory of the most high God, and that my neighbour may be benefited thereby." That is what I would have liked to say about my work.'[35]

Part II
Philosophy

Chapter 3
Wittgenstein and Philosophy

In order to show the distinct nature of Wittgenstein's philosophy it is worthwhile to contrast it with the philosophy of Descartes, Locke and Berkeley. It is clearly outside the scope of this discussion to evaluate their philosophies comprehensively. Instead, the following brief discussion of these philosophers provides a general understanding of their positions as a background to show Wittgenstein's thought in relief. In general, I want to show that, in contrast to Wittgenstein, these philosophers ultimately place a precedent upon our ideas and consequently distance and diminish the world we live in. Descartes creates an epistemological distance between the private thinker and the external world, Locke distances the substance of the world from the observer via connections of various qualities, and Berkeley collapses the world into the individual's mind.

This particular focus fits a discussion of Wittgenstein's philosophy since his central concern is how language connects to reality. Does language connect to a reality that is independent and external to it (Locke and linguistic realism)? Does language make its own reality (Berkeley and linguistic idealism)? Wittgenstein's early philosophy has some similarities with the former realism, while some commentators place his later thought in the latter category. I will argue that Wittgenstein's philosophy does not side with realism or idealism – despite the fact that realism and idealism are often presented as the only two options.

In contrast to realism and idealism, Wittgenstein's later philosophy shows how language is internally connected to life (in contrast to the casual external connections of realism) and how what language discusses is nonetheless an external reality (in contrast to idealism). However, to see this point correctly it is very useful, as discussed above, to trace the problem back out of the fly bottle and thereby address the tradition of philosophy he breaks from and argues (at least implicitly) against; namely, scepticism, realism and idealism.

Descartes

Descartes (1596–1650) received his education at the College of La Fleche under Jesuit educators. Thus, his education was within the scholastic tradition of integrating Aristotle with theology. God gave humans reason and therefore truths reached by reason are reconcilable with theology in a metaphysical system. Descartes continues with an emphasis on reason, but begins to search more deeply for truth and certainty. He turns from the scholastic tradition, which he considers to be stuck in closed technical arguments and jargon, to search for certainty. He notes, 'Regarding philosophy, I shall say only this: seeing that it has been cultivated for many centuries by the most excellent minds and yet there is still no point in it which is not disputed and hence doubtful.'[36] Descartes wants to replace the scholastic method with one of a more certain nature to provide a secure foundation for knowledge, where every assertion will rest on its proof and no proof would rest on assumptions. Consequently, he tears down the traditional scholastic structure to build from a new foundation of clear and distinct ideas with the tools of reason alone.

Descartes is thereby regarded as the founder of modern philosophy in general and of a method in particular. His method is found in the classic work *Meditations on First Philosophy* (1641). He advances the claim that his education and experience have not provided him with the means to secure knowledge. Therefore, he begins anew to be certain that each move he makes follows what is secure, that no one part of his knowledge rests on uncertain grounds. Rather than trusting anything, he doubts everything. Hence, his method of doubt clears what he regards as the very shaky knowledge that has previously been built in order to clear the way for a more secure foundation that can guarantee the rationality of what is built upon it.

Once he has levelled previous knowledge to the ground through the method of doubt he turns to reason as the tool to begin his building project. Knowledge is typically thought to be derived from at least one of two paths, we can gain knowledge through our innate ideas or we gain knowledge through our senses. The former is rationalism and the latter is empiricism. Descartes maintains that the mind alone can discover truth apart from empirical experience. Whether or not Descartes can truly be categorized a rationalist may be open to debate; however, the reason he is considered to be a rationalist is a consequence of doubting all knowledge derived from the senses until he ends up with his reason alone.

Descartes begins his quest for knowledge with a rejection of the senses since they can deceive us. His method is one of leading the mind away from the senses since 'the senses deceive, and it is prudent never to trust completely those who have deceived us even once.'[37] Most people agree that our senses can mislead us at some point in our lives, but Descartes takes the sceptic's doubt as far as he can. A global sceptic will hold that we cannot know anything with certainty. Perhaps you are dreaming that you are reading this sentence. Perhaps you are a concoction of chemicals in a test tube being stimulated to have the experience of reading this sentence. Maybe the world as you know it came into existence 30 minutes ago. Descartes even denies the certainty of mathematical and logical truths. An invisible demon may be tricking you into believing that $2 + 2 = 4$. He notes that a 'malicious demon of the utmost power and cunning' may have the purpose of deceiving him. It is thereby possible that 'the sky, the earth, colours, shapes, sounds and all external things are merely the delusions of dreams which he has devised to ensnare my judgement.'[38]

Because the senses are not reliable, Descartes eventually whittled his way down to the mind, the last item on Descartes' list of things to doubt and remove. What about that malicious demon, surely he cannot trust reason. However, what he discovers is that not even an evil demon can remove this last standing item on his list. Descartes notes, 'Let the demon deceive me as much as he may . . . *I am, I exist* is necessarily true whenever it is put forward by me or conceived in my mind.'[39] Even if the evil demon deceives you, it is still you who is thinking about being deceived! It is useful to quote Descartes in full:

> Since I now wish to devote myself solely to the search for truth, I thought it necessary to . . . reject as if absolutely false everything in which I could imagine the least doubt, in order to see if I was left believing anything that was entirely indubitable. Thus because our senses sometimes deceive us, I decided to suppose that nothing was such as they led us to imagine. And since there are men who make mistakes in reasoning, committing logical fallacies concerning the simplest questions in geometry, and because I judged that I was as prone to error as anyone else, I rejected as unsound all the arguments I had previously taken as demonstrative proofs. Lastly, considering that the very thoughts we have while awake may also occur while we sleep without any of them being at that time true, I resolved to pretend that all the things that had ever entered my mind were no more true than the illusions of my dreams. But immediately I noticed that while I was trying thus to think everything false, it was necessary that I, who was thinking this, was something. And observing that this truth 'I am thinking, therefore I exist' was so firm and sure that all the most extravagant suppositions of the sceptics were incapable of shaking it, I decided that I could accept it without scruple as the first principle of the philosophy I was seeking.[40]

This is where the infamous '*Cogito ergo Sum*' is reached, 'I am thinking, therefore I exist.' In other words, you cannot doubt doubt. This is Descartes' Archimedean point, that is, the foundation that he can now build upon from the inside out.

Descartes uses his 'clear and distinct' rule to build upon this one foundation of the *Cogito ergo Sum*. However, he needs to avoid the invisible demon that may place ideas in one's mind, and he needs to steer away from solipsism. Maybe he is the only thinking person that exists, perhaps all the other seeming people in the world are only automatons. His answer to these problems is God, and he is certain that there is a God since something causes the idea of God to be in his mind, a cause must be as real as is its effect, and his idea of God did not come from nowhere; therefore, God exists. Descartes writes,

> I see plainly that the certainty and truth of all knowledge depends uniquely on my awareness of the true God, to such an extent that I was incapable of perfect knowledge about anything else until I became aware of him. And now it is possible for me to achieve full and certain knowledge of countless matters, both concerning God himself and other things whose nature is intellectual, and also concerning the whole of that corporeal nature which is the subject-matter of pure mathematics.[41]

Descartes' argument for the existence of God is not along the traditional arguments that move from observations within the world to God as the cause of those effects, but it is still casual, that is, the effects are in the mind since God places the idea of himself within our minds.[42] Moreover, the cause of a perfect idea (in an imperfect mind) must itself be perfect (Third Meditation). With God secure in his thought he can build knowledge since, in contrast to the demon, God is perfect and truthful, not a deceiver. Consequently, there is an external world that appears to us without the demon's deceptions (Sixth Meditation). Although Descartes grants that there is an external world, the foundation he builds from is not the external world. He concludes that there is knowledge of the external world by beginning with the foundation of his mind.

Descartes moves from what he regards as the probable basis of the scholastic arguments to premises whose truth we can intuit; meaning, for Descartes, that which is rationally apprehended in contrast to that which is seen with ones eyes. He says,

> by 'intuition' I do not mean the fluctuating testimony of the senses or the deceptive judgment of the imagination as it botches things together, but the conception of a clear and attentive mind, which is so easy and distinct that there can be no room for doubt about what we are

understanding . . . intuition is the indubitable conception
of a clear and attentive mind which proceeds solely
from the light of reason . . . thus everyone can mentally
intuit that he exists, that he is thinking, that a triangle
is bounded by just three sides and a sphere is a single
surface, and the like.[43]

Descartes method depends on the *lux naturae*, the light of nature
that enables the individual to reject the misleading senses and
discover the essential structure of reality.

Consequently, Descartes provides a dualistic conception of
humans – the physical and the mental. He maintains the following: that I think cannot be doubted, that I have a body can
be doubted; therefore, existence is based on thinking and the
essence of a person is thinking. Descartes' method rests on a
denial of flesh and blood humans, 'this "I" . . . is entirely distinct from the body, and indeed is easier to know than the body,
and would not fail to be whatever it is, even if the body did not
exist.'[44] Given the focus on innate knowledge we should ask,
'Can a new born baby reflect on metaphysics?' If the senses are
not what provide knowledge, then surely the infants mind has
this innate knowledge. Descartes apparently accepts this consequence of his theory, albeit admitting, as Plato did, that the
infant's body is so overwhelmed by stimuli that it may not find
the time to concentrate on metaphysics. Descartes notes, 'It seems
reasonable to think that a mind newly united to an infant's body
is wholly occupied in perceiving or feeling the ideas of pain,
pleasure, heat, cold and other similar ideas which arise from its
union and intermingling with the body.' Moreover, 'I have no
doubt that if it were released from the prison of the body, it
would find them within itself'.[45] We do not acquire these ideas
later on, as we grow older. Whatever the status of the newborn
is, Descartes clearly notes, 'The body is always a hindrance to
the mind in its thinking, and this was especially true in youth.'[46]
In contrast to Descartes, Rebecca Pentz rightly notes that the
core Judaeo-Christian view of the soul is quite at odds with the
views of Plato and Descartes. The word usually translated 'soul'
comes from the word for breath, *nephesh*, and is used primar-
ily to denote the whole living being. Far from being identified

with consciousness or mental life, the *nephesh* can be hungry and thirsty (Ps. 107.5). [47]

Descartes does admit that 'I am not merely present in the body as a sailor is present in a ship; but that I am very closely joined and, as it were, intermingled with it, so that I and the body form a unit.'[48] Nevertheless, the dualism between the physical senses and the mind in Descartes' work leads him to devalue the former as animated machines (i.e. not conscious, but mechanical automata without sensory awareness) to the extreme point of regarding dissected animals making painful cries as nothing other than the inevitable sounds made by a machine being dismantled – not the sounds of pain. At best, he posited the pineal gland as the location or nexus of the body and mind unit, but simply describing a mysterious body part does not guarantee that a mind has knowledge of the external world. The relation between the incorporeal self and the mechanical body remains a quagmire, and does not seem to provide the guarantees sought – at least not without God.

The well-known problem with Descartes' method is the 'Cartesian Circle'. Descartes needs God to guarantee his method and the method to guarantee God. For example, I have the clear and distinct idea of God, therefore God exists, and God guarantees the clear and distinct idea, *ad nauseam* in a circle. If the existence of God is required to guarantee the reliability of clear and distinct ideas, then how can the idea of God be reliable in the first place? Ultimately, it is a bit of a paradox that Descartes aims to arrive at a clear understanding of the physical world, but to do so he retreats from the physical world. In other words, he ends up opening the door to further scepticism as he opens the epistemological chasm between the mind and the external world, and actually provides a foundation that is a metaphysical quicksand that only God can pull him out of. Descartes, like Plato before him, sees true knowledge as residing in an abstract and intellectual realm, in contrast to the secondary fleeting material world. He appears to turn from the Aristotelian tradition back to the earlier Platonic conception of philosophy.

The epistemological problems that Descartes opens can lead to either realism or idealism, both of which are attempts to show how we do have knowledge without falling into scepticism. We will look briefly at the theories of Locke (realism) and Berkeley (idealism). The former sustains the separation between our ideas and the external world but regards the senses as generally reliable, while the latter collapses the separation and thereby negates the need to explain the link between the ideas and the external world. In any case, it is un-Wittgensteinian to imagine that solitary reason can start from scratch and rebuild knowledge; instead, Wittgenstein will show that human knowledge is by necessity bound to language and social conditions and we cannot step outside of these to reach an Archimedean point.

Locke and realism

The English philosopher John Locke (1632–1704) is a key empiricist philosopher. Like Descartes, he wanted to find the secure foundation of knowledge. Locke notes in his most read work, *An Essay Concerning Human Understanding* (1689): 'My purpose', he says, 'is to enquire into the origin, certainty, and extent of human knowledge; together, with the grounds and degrees of belief, opinion, and assent.'[49] Towards this goal he was indebted to Descartes, to whom he owed 'the great obligation of my first deliverance from the unintelligible way of talking of the philosophy in use in the schools'[50]; namely, the Aristotelian scholasticism.

Locke credits Descartes with helping him to break from scholastic thought, but he rejects rationalism and turns to empiricism. As one of the first empiricist opponents of Descartes, he puts the theory of innate ideas to the test and rejects it. In contrast to Descartes and rationalism he says,

> It is an established opinion amongst men that there are in
> the understanding certain innate principles, some primary
> notions . . . characters as it were stamped upon the mind
> of man, which the soul receives at its very first being,
> and brings into the world with it. It would be sufficient
> to convince unprejudiced readers of the falseness of this
> supposition if I could only show (as I hope I shall in the
> following parts of this Discourse) how men . . . may

attain to all the knowledge they have without the help of any innate impressions. . . .[51]

Since knowledge does not come from innate ideas, it follows that knowledge is acquired from the senses. Indeed, Locke notes: 'There is nothing in the intellect that wasn't previously in the senses.' We do not have innate ideas (knowledge of mathematical truths, universals, etc.); instead, the mind is a blank slate (*tabula rasa*).[52] Locke writes, 'Let us suppose the mind to be, as we say, white paper, void of all characters, without any ideas; how comes it to be furnished? . . . Whence has it all the materials of reason and knowledge? To this I answer, in one word, from *experience*.'[53] For Locke, the mind is a recipient of experience and acquires knowledge; it is not a storehouse of innate knowledge.

Since we gain knowledge through the senses, the Cartesian innatism and rationalism are replaced by a more naturalistic theory. More specifically, what Locke ends up with is representationalism (in contrast to a naive realism of perceiving reality directly so that the mind literally mirrors an external reality). The real world causes our perceptions by representing the physical world through sense data, which are mental entities that are private to each individual perceiver. This is a causal theory of perception, a process whereby the external world strikes the perceiver's sense organs and sends a message to the brain where they are mental events. Hence, knowledge is not merely manifested from the senses; rather, experience based ideas are the building blocks that reason uses to build knowledge. This represents a type of atomism since the ultimate building blocks of knowledge are simple perceptual units (simple ideas) combined into a compound of these ideas and their relation to each other. For example, the colour orange and geometric shapes such as a sphere are simples that can be built into the compound that forms our knowledge of an orange. Clearly, this causal process is mechanical and supposes that there really is an orange; you are not just dreaming that there is an orange. However, even though Locke is a realist and assumes that there is a physical external world, he nonetheless ends with a non-physical result; namely, the mental event of sense impression.

Locke's empiricism assumes that all we can experience are representations of the world, and in particular two distinct qualities: primary and secondary. Primary qualities are in the object itself while secondary qualities are in the mind and not in the object. Hence, primary qualities are true representations of the object they represent since they are inseparable from the object, examples being extension, solidity, number, movement, rest, etc, which are the unquestioned features of the physical world. For example, we know that the orange has a spherical shape. Primary qualities are thereby measurable using numbers and are the same for everyone. Secondary qualities, however, are not in the physical object. Instead, they are caused by the primary qualities and are things such as colour, sensations, smell, etc., that cause the sensations and perceptions in the perceiver. For example, if you look at an orange the colour you see is not in the physical object; rather, it is a reflection off the physical objects primary quality that causes this particular reflection of orangeness. We are never fully aware of the object in and of itself, only the idea or representation of the object. So secondary qualities do not show the world as it is, only as the world appears to be for each individual privately. If there were aliens, and if they travelled to our world, then it would be possible on Locke's account that although they would still experience an orange as a sphere (primary quality), it may have a different colour and taste due to the nature of secondary qualities. In short: secondary qualities produce sensations and primary qualities cause the secondary qualities.

Behind all the qualities is substance, the foundation of matter and the source of reality underlying the mental event produced through experience. It should be clear, however, that no one, except for God, could actually perceive or have full knowledge of this underlying stratum; it is simply too far removed from the casual process. The only direct and unmediated experience we have is our private ideas that represent the external world. As Locke notes, the mind 'perceives nothing but its own *ideas*'.[54] Therefore, a chasm is created between private perceptions and their object. Locke cannot claim that we know substance since all knowledge comes from the senses and we have no sensation of substance (only of the qualities). Therefore, Locke calls this underlying foundation of substance 'something I know not what'. The something he knows not what is nonetheless predicated as the foundation of our reality.

Despite the clear differences between Descartes and Locke, it would be wrong to regard them as completely at odds with each other simply because the former is labelled a rationalist and the latter an empiricist. Locke rightly wants to maintain the independence and reality of the physical world (realism) since it is the source of our ideas and knowledge, but he maintains the problematic Cartesian separation between our ideas and the physical world. Both Locke and Descartes limit perception to the contents of our own mind.

Wittgenstein's *Tractatus Logico-Philosophicus* and realism

It is appropriate to discuss Wittgenstein's early work at this point since it, like Locke's philosophy, can be associated with realism. Locke's connection of words to things is secondary (indirect) rather than primary:

> Words, as they are used by Men, can properly and
> immediately signify nothing but the *Ideas* that are in the
> Mind of the speaker; yet they in their thoughts give them
> secret reference to two other things. First, they suppose
> their Words to be marks of the Ideas in the Minds also
> of other Men . . . Secondly . . . they often suppose their
> Words to stand also for the reality of things.[55]

The immediate signification of a word is the speaker's private idea; therefore, there is a great distance between one's idea and what the word signifies. Nonetheless, for Locke, there must be a reality that is not dependent on our ideas and words since without such independence our words and knowledge would be arbitrary.

We tend to assume that the relation between language and reality is one where the latter is the independent ground for language. This is an important basis of realism since it assumes that it counteracts the problem of relativism and scepticism. That there is a uniformity and independence of reality is, for the realist, akin to the linguistic realist's claim that language also rests on the uniformity of reality. Locke's philosophy and Wittgenstein's early philosophy regard language as grounded on an independent reality that it must reflect. Consequently, the relation between reality and language is independent and external.

Wittgenstein's early work tries to determine the relation between propositions, the structure of reality, and ultimately logic, in order to determine sense. That is, what is the nature of language mirroring an independent and external reality? In particular, the say and show distinction was integral to his early thought whereby we must understand what can be legitimately said, as compared to what can only be shown. What can be said is compared to a hieroglyphic writing 'which pictures the facts it describes'.[56] Likewise, propositions picture the world and are thereby a 'picture of reality'.[57] For example, the proposition 'my kayak is on my car' pictures the fact that my kayak is on my car. We can understand this proposition and it makes sense because it is a possible state of affairs. We could, however, change the proposition to 'my car is on my kayak' and we still equally understand what is said. The picture is reversed (and perhaps my kayak is squashed!). In both cases, the proposition and the world relate to each other, in other words, the proposition pictures reality by being a logical map of a possible state of affairs that can be verified by comparing the propositional picture with reality. So in contrast to Locke's associations, Wittgenstein wants to show that the relation between language and reality can be understood as a pictorial relation, a type of geometrical projection.

Propositions that are a possible state of affairs have sense and can be said; all of which necessarily fit together since there is a link between the proposition and reality. It is significant that the above propositions – 'my kayak is on my car' and 'my car is on my kayak' – make sense even without knowing which one, if either, is true. The sense of a proposition is independent of its truth or falsehood, but importantly it must be true or false. That is, it must be able to express something about the world. If the proposition cannot be true or false, then it is either senseless or nonsense. For example, the proposition 'kayak headaches are red' is not false, it is nonsense. There is no geometrical projection that can be applied.

Wittgenstein does not leave his analysis at this level; he goes much deeper. Propositions can be broken down into smaller pieces starting with elementary propositions. Complex propositions, such as 'my kayak is on my car', are truth functions of elementary propositions (which are truth functions of themselves) and are thereby determined in sense by elementary propositions which are in turn composed of names. Names come into direct contact with the world since they link with the world *via* a simple object. The name with this link substitutes for the simple object and can take its place.[58] The point here is that complex propositions can be true or false, and this can be determined by looking at the world to see if it is true or false. Consequently, if the complex proposition 'my kayak is on top of my car' is true, then the proposition 'my car is on top of my kayak' is false. However, elementary propositions, which are concatenations of names for simple objects, have a different order of logic since names must make contact with the world, they must name something, and if they do not name something then they have no meaning. In other words, it is possible to have a false complex proposition, but it is impossible to have a false name since it must necessarily connect with a simple object.

The terms in a complex proposition, such as kayak, are not names or simple objects. A kayak can be broken down into simpler parts and ultimately each part of the kayak is then in a relation to each other and to the car. This process of logical analysis begins with the complex and ends at the name and its simple object that connects to reality. So what is an example of an elementary proposition, name and simple object? Well, Wittgenstein never gave such an example due to the considerably complex and difficult (impossible) task it entailed to arrive at the underlying logical syntax. Nevertheless he writes, 'it does not go against our feeling, that *we* cannot analyse propositions so far to mention the elements by name; no, we feel that the world must consist of elements.'[59] The simple object not only secures meaning, Wittgenstein posits a limit to their number to avoid an infinite regress of possible facts: 'For the totality of facts determines both what is the case, and also all that is not the case,'[60] moreover, 'the specification of all true elementary propositions describes the world completely,'[61] and the 'totality of propositions is the language.'[62] Thus, the possible configurations of simple objects are the boundary of language. Wittgenstein posits the simple object in order to determine sense, to resist the problem of relativism, and to secure a connection to reality – no further propositions are required. This is what can be said, it is the limit of language, and beyond which there is nothing for the name to link with.

In summary: Wittgenstein's early work, in realist fashion, supports the idea that language has external causal connections along with the empiricist view of language. Hence, a real proposition represents a possibility in logical space and has a mode of verification; namely, symbolic logic that guides us to its truth and shows that we also understand the proposition. Propositions (which are in a projective relation to reality) are constructed on a geometrical basis and the sense of the proposition is a function of names that stand directly for objects. Consequently, there is a separation between the elements that make the proposition and the proposition itself, that is, the complex proposition is composed of smaller elements and ultimately the simple object. The sense that a proposition has is completely independent of human convention; in other words, anyone who could see the proposition with super-human vision down to its structure would understand its meaning – there is no room for interpretation since the projective relation connects names directly to simple objects.

What is shown, in contrast to what can be said, is beyond propositions and is transcendental. Whereas a proposition must be a possible state of affairs in the world, the transcendental is not a state of affairs in the world and is therefore not sayable. Since the shown is not sayable it follows that crossing the boundary of possible states of affairs into the transcendental with names will incur confusion. Hence, Wittgenstein writes, 'What we cannot speak about we must pass over in silence.'[63] We must heed to the limit of language and not cross over into the shown; namely, logic, but also value, ethics and religion.

It is wrong to assume that Wittgenstein, even in his early work, is thereby a positivist who denies any validity to what is beyond what can be said. Engelmann rightly notes:

> A whole generation of disciples was able to take
> Wittgenstein for a positivist because he has something of
> enormous importance in common with the positivists:
> he draws the line between what we can speak about
> and what we must be silent about just as they do. The
> difference is only that they have nothing to be silent
> about. Positivism holds – and this is its essence – that
> what we can speak about is all that matters in life.
> *Whereas Wittgenstein passionately believes that all that really*
> *matters in human life is precisely what, in his view, we must*
> *be silent about.* When he nevertheless takes immense
> pains to delimit the unimportant, it is not the coastline
> of that island which he is bent on surveying with such
> meticulous accuracy, but the boundary of the ocean.[64]

Just because Wittgenstein regards the shown as unsayable it does not follow that it is pointless or insignificant. Indeed, that which is passed over in silence (the shown) is the most significant – it is senseless, not nonsense (e.g. kayaks have red headaches). The shown is given a significance that it could not have if it was only another state of affairs within the world.

Wittgenstein says, 'We now have to answer *a priori* the question about all the possible forms of elementary propositions.'[65] He is seeking the essence of the proposition, to find what all propositions have in common, and to combat relativism. Just as Locke posits the uniformity of nature, so Wittgenstein posits a uniform logic. That propositions link with the world and that language and reality have a common structure is evident, but propositions do not and cannot explain this relationship. To be able to explain it would involve the impossible task of stepping outside logic and the world with our propositions. The connection between language and the world is one of a pre-established harmony and Wittgenstein calls this shown but unspeakable link between language and reality 'logical form'.

It is important to see that logical form is not an addition to propositions and reality, as if it is a third category that acts as some kind of glue to hold everything together; rather, it is simply shown in this relationship. Logical form enables propositions to be said – true or false – and while it permeates everything that is sayable (it is the one logic of language) it says nothing itself of what is in the world. The shown points to an *a priori* order in the world that is a logical form that says nothing, is independent of the empirical, yet it is necessary for anything to be said of the empirical (e.g. while what can be said, as is found in science, does speak of what is in the world).

This *a priori* status of Wittgenstein's logical form (an external stricture to which language must adhere) ties his early work back to Platonic realism in light of the similarity between Wittgenstein's simple objects and Plato's Forms. In the *Tractatus* language has a logical space that is similar to the Platonic Forms since language must submit to these external and immutable frames. Yet it is important to note that although there is a type of Platonic realism in Wittgenstein's early conception of logic he sees reality as internal to logic where the simple object is part of the world, while the Platonic Forms are outside the world. Nonetheless, even if logic does not have a foundation outside the world, it is still a metaphysical foundation of language that takes precedence over the practice and use of language. Logical form gives meaning to signs in our language, not according to convention (convention may determine the look of the sign), but according to the logical structure of the world.

For Wittgenstein there is an underlying logical syntax behind our everyday language. He notes that 'language disguises thought; so that from the external form of the clothes one cannot infer the form of thought they clothe, because the external form of the clothes is constructed with quite another object than to let the body be recognized'[66] – and for Plato there is an ideal intelligibility behind our changing world. Despite the difference between a Tractarian and Platonic formal unity, neither are open to plain view in our fleeting world – who can see the Forms or simple objects?

Wittgenstein's early work does not entirely dismiss the application of language in order to grasp its meaning, but he certainly places less significance on it compared to his later thought. Instead, he emphasizes the underlying logical structure of language – that is hidden by ordinary language – and the resultant analysis of the logical connection between complex propositions, elementary propositions, and finally names and simple objects.

We can now see a similarity between the rationalist Descartes who separates the mind from the physical and human world, the empiricist Locke who separates ideas from the substance of the world, and the early Wittgenstein who separates logic from the conventions of the human world – they all create categories that either distance the human world, or question the human world. Descartes' *cogito ergo sum*, Locke's unknown something, and Wittgenstein's simple objects are all vastly different, but they are metaphysical foundations that take precedence over concrete human activities.

Berkeley and idealism

Berkeley (1685–1753) was an Irish philosopher and Anglican bishop who received his education from Trinity College, Dublin. His thought is not similar to Wittgenstein; indeed, it is unique in the tradition of philosophy. Yet it represents an important instance of distancing our ideas from the concrete world. He agrees with Descartes and Locke that what we immediately experience are our own ideas. However, Berkeley rejects their methods since they imply scepticism. How could someone who is aware only of his or her own ideas know anything about the external world? So how does Berkeley agree with Descartes and Locke that we only experience our own ideas yet avoid the resultant scepticism concerning the external world? He rejects an independent external world!

Scepticism asks whether reality is accessible to human knowledge and whether reality is only a human creation. Realism responds to the former question affirmatively, while idealism responds to the latter affirmatively. Whereas Locke and Wittgenstein in realist fashion think that our ideas and language mirror an independent and external reality, Berkeley espouses idealism and thinks that reality mirrors our ideas and language.

For example, Locke uses the term 'idea' to designate intermediaries between the mind and the external world. In contrast, Berkeley's theory holds that since we only have ideas we perceive things directly without any intermediary steps. This addresses the problem of Locke's unknown something behind our perceptions by removing the distance and distinction between our private ideas and the external world.

Berkeley's seemingly drastic idea is not simply a new theory; rather, it can be viewed as the logical conclusion of Locke's theory. According to Berkeley, Locke's representationalism – that our perceptions resemble physical objects and can be divided into primary and secondary qualities – is unsound since without the secondary quality of orange for an orange you cannot understand its primary quality of being a sphere. Moreover, since we only experience ideas there is no distinction between primary and secondary qualities outside of us because we only have ideas inside of us. Locke's physical objects/qualities are thought to have the ability to cause ideas of sensible qualities, but we then have no idea of matter itself – it is this conception of matter that Berkeley rightly wants to reject.

Berkeley says, 'let anyone consider those arguments, which are thought manifestly to prove that colours and tastes exist only in the mind, and he shall find they may, with equal force, be brought to prove the same thing of extension, figure and motion.'[67] Since only ideas are perceived it follows that what we cannot see is invisible (Locke's unknown somewhat), but how can we have a representation of something that is invisible? What is the difference between 'something I know not what' and nothing at all? If we only get ideas from experience, and Locke's matter is an unknown something, Berkeley concludes that matter does not exist. For Berkeley, this is the logical conclusion of Locke's theory since even he believed that we are not aware of anything but our ideas. Berkeley rejects Locke's primary and secondary quality distinction, that the essential nature of matter is extension, and his understanding of substance. In contrast, Berkeley thinks that the essential aspect of matter is our perceiving it. Indeed, he says 'to exist is to be perceived' (*Esse est percipi*).

Berkeley notes that to cause is to act; therefore, since only the mind and will are active, it follows that Locke's inanimate material bodies cannot cause anything. According to Berkeley, there is nothing represented; rather, physical objects are nothing more than mental events. Idealism holds that since the mind's ideas constitute reality and the connection between the external and internal world is therefore not inductive (e.g. as Locke assumes), it then follows through deduction that physical objects are ideas. Berkeley reduces matter to ideas since the so-called physical object is actually an idea. His answer to the problems within Locke's theory was to deny the existence of matter to avoid Locke's definition of matter as an 'unknown somewhat' and to reject the claim that the mind is dependent on an external and independent physical world. In short: Berkeley rejects Locke's mechanical world-view and materialism and replaces it with immaterialism.

So how can my house and dog continue to exist if I do not perceive them? The answer is that God continually perceives everything. The apparent continuity we take for granted (e.g. the fire in my fireplace will continue to warm my room even if I am not present to perceive it) is a result of God's continuing perception. Interestingly, Locke and Berkeley agree that statements about sensible qualities are about ideas, but they have different foundations for ideas. Berkeley's immaterialism is the result of starting with Locke's theory but he replaces matter with God. For Locke matter gives rise to ideas, whereas for Berkley God is ultimately the foundation to guarantee continuity, knowledge and ideas. Berkeley says, 'Theology and philosophy gently unbind the ligaments that chain the soul down to earth, and assist her flight toward the sovereign Good. There is an instinct or tendency of the mind upwards which sheweth a natural endeavour to recover and raise ourselves from our present sensual and low condition, into a state of light, order, purity.'[68] His theory certainly takes a metaphysical flight and removes us perhaps even further from the world. Berkeley draws Locke's method to its logical conclusion, but he leaves us within our ideas as we began with Descartes.

Chapter 4

Wittgenstein's Later Philosophy

In the *Tractatus* Wittgenstein notes,

> The right method of philosophy would be this. To say
> nothing except what can be said . . . and then always,
> when someone else wished to say something metaphysical,
> to demonstrate to him that he had given no meaning to
> certain signs in his propositions. This method would be
> unsatisfactory to the other – he would not have the feeling
> that we were teaching him philosophy – but it would be
> the only strictly correct method.[69]

In his later work, *Philosophical Investigations*, Wittgenstein says, 'What is your aim in philosophy? – To show the fly the way out of the fly-bottle.'[70] In both his early and later work, Wittgenstein wants to show the way out of confusion (the fly bottle). To this end, his early work rejects metaphysics by tying language to an underlying logical syntax. His later work also rejects metaphysics – but now *including* the underlying logical syntax.

That there is a shift in his work after the *Tractatus* is clear. Wittgenstein says, 'It suddenly seemed to me that I should publish those old thoughts and the new ones together: that the latter could be seen in the right light only by contrast with and against the background of my old way of thinking.'[71] What is debated is how radical this shift from the old to the new is. What I want to make clear is that Wittgenstein moves from placing logic underneath language, to seeing logic revealed and shown in the applications of language. Consequently, by the time of *On Certainty* it is clear that he is not emphasizing epistemology and what we can and cannot say based on an underlying logical syntax, but what we do say. He turns away from hidden metaphysical foundations towards our ordinary everyday lives where logic is revealed in language.

Scepticism

Wittgenstein's later work turns to the shown and revealed nature of logic and language that we have in our everyday lives. The ideas that we are removed from the world as solitary observers and that ultimately there is a primary foundation outside our secondary every day experience is rejected. What he also rejects, consequently, is scepticism. For the sceptic, the mind is a passive recipient of uncertain data that we cannot convincingly link with the external world. The sceptic sees the rather fleeting sense-data link between the external world and the mind and asks the obvious question; namely, 'how can I ever know or accurately describe reality?' Wittgenstein stops scepticism in its tracks, not by winning the fight against it by positing further theories to provide a better explanation of how we can have knowledge, but by denying that the sceptics are even putting up a fight.

Without the distance created by Descartes between the mind and the external world, and without the theories of Locke and Berkley to deal with this distance, Wittgenstein simply notes, 'God grant the philosopher insight into what lies in front of everyone's eyes.'[72] He is not using God as a foundation or guarantee of knowledge; instead, it is a simple request to focus on common sense. What Wittgenstein's later work shows is that metaphysical foundations are an illusion (and can therefore be doubted), but our everyday lives and convention of carrying on the way we do cannot be doubted, but not because his theory secures meaning. Rather, it makes no sense to raise doubts once we have rejected the theories that lead to doubt in the first place.

The sceptic's questions move from particular examples, our senses can sometimes deceive us, to a general sceptical conclusion; we can never trust our senses. However, in our everyday lives we typically take empirical facts for granted. For example, we see a tree in the park, while at the same time the sceptic wants to say that the empirical evidence that you see a tree is not reliable. We expect the world to vary from our differing perspectives so that what may appear to be a small tree is actually large, we agree that physical objects look different from different angles, distances and conditions. However, if the size of a tree is deceptive in some conditions, such as a snow storm, then why move from that case of doubtful circumstances to doubt all circumstances? In any case, the sceptic often goes beyond real examples and ends by saying knowledge is not rightly tied to empirical propositions since they *could* turn out to be false.

If empirical propositions cannot be trusted because they could be distorted or wrong, then is there any knowledge and certainty? The sceptic's answer is yes, in logic and mathematics. For example, 'A is A' is a necessary proposition and is therefore true, in contrast to 'A is not A'. Unlike contingent empirical propositions, these remain true. For example, if I am typing at my desk in my room I could say 'there is a desk in my room'. However, according to the sceptic, because the contradictory statement 'there is not a desk in my room' makes sense, it then follows that my original statement can never be classified as knowledge. Conversely, 'A is A' and '1 + 1 = 2' will always be true and their contradictory statements never make sense; therefore, 'A is A' and '1 + 1 = 2' are certain. However, does this really make sense? Could I ever say, 'there is not a desk in my room' while typing at my desk? Is it reasonable to conclude – while typing at my desk in my room – that there may not actually be a desk in my room since the contradictory statement 'there is not a desk in my room' in abstraction makes sense? No, it is meaningless. The problem is that the contradictory of my original statement regarding the desk in my room has no application. Wittgenstein notes: 'I am sitting with a philosopher in the garden; he says again and again "I know that that's a tree," pointing to a tree that is near us. Someone else arrives and hears this, and I tell him: "This fellow isn't insane. We are doing philosophy."'[73] These are the sorts of problems we fall into once language and meaning are removed from their context. The problem is that the logic of knowledge and certainty in one discussion, 'A is A' for example, is placed on the logic of another, 'there is a desk in my room' (empirical propositions). Doubt then becomes abstracted from all applications so that nothing can ultimately satisfy the sceptic, and consequently human knowledge is always questionable.

We need to see that knowledge and certainty have their place in empirical discourse, albeit obviously different than in logical discourse. Wittgenstein agrees with the sceptic that there cannot be an absolute guarantee, but argues that no guarantee is needed for our everyday language and meaning, there is no need to refute scepticism. The virus does not need to be argued with, so to speak, it needs to be eliminated. What Wittgenstein eliminates is the sceptic's pointless questions. For example, if I see a tree in my yard, should I listen to the sceptic and doubt it, or is this beyond doubt? Wittgenstein notes:

> If 'I know etc.' is conceived as a grammatical proposition, of course the 'I' cannot be important. And it properly means 'There is no such thing as a doubt in this case' or 'The expression "I do not know" makes no sense in this case.' And of course it follows from this that 'I *know*' makes no sense either.[74]

If I say that I know there is a tree in my yard, what gives this certainty is not a theory regarding how I know this; indeed, to go beyond the given incurs even greater scepticism. That there is a tree in my yard is not subject to doubt because it plays a role in my life, I water it, walk around it, etc., in which case doubt is not refuted – it is nonsensical. Would it make sense to say I do not know that there is a tree in my back yard as I walk around it and water it? Wittgenstein gives up any notion of arguing against scepticism and instead he simply regards the sceptic's words as nonsense.

The sceptic's doubts are not answered with another theory, such as Berkeley's, to show how we *can* know reality, but instead shows how we *do* know reality – a reality that is not based on our private ideas and language. It is not by turning away from the world that a guarantee of knowledge is discovered, it is this turning from the world that incurs further trouble. In the *Tractatus* Wittgenstein writes: 'Scepticism is not irrefutable, but palpably senseless, if it would doubt where a question cannot be asked.'[75] By seeing the unintelligibility of scepticism, the intelligibility of our ordinary experiences is more clearly seen. Rather than being lead to concerns over the nature of reality and the existence of a tree in your yard, and how you can know the difference between an imaginary tree and a real tree, Wittgenstein points out how we do know the difference – we water the real one. Language and reality are by nature social and interactive, and as such, the notion that we are solitary thinkers working out correlations between words/ideas and objects is rejected.

Philosophical Investigations

What is the nature of knowledge and certainty if it does not need to meet the sceptic's standards? How does Wittgenstein embed meaning within our world in contrast to relying upon external strictures? Recall that the early Wittgenstein, in the *Tractatus*, thinks of language as tied to an independent reality, and logical form gives meaning to signs in our language, not convention, according to the logical structure of the world. So language amounts to using the sign logically. Logical form underlies our language to ensure meaning and the link between the world and the form of language is set in a pre-established harmony.

In *Philosophical Investigations,* Wittgenstein shows the shift from his former atomistic conception of meaning; that is, he rejects the idea that a proposition is whatever can be true or false, as if what is true or false determines what is or is not a proposition.[76] Wittgenstein was unsatisfied with the idea that philosophers can work out the logical possibility and impossibility of what can be said. Indeed, he becomes dissatisfied with the idea of any theory to explain language:

> Formerly, I myself spoke of a 'complete analysis', and I used to believe that philosophy had to give a definite dissection of propositions so as to set out clearly all their connections and remove all possibility of misunderstanding. I spoke as if there were a calculus in which such a dissection would be possible . . . At the root of all this there was a false and idealized picture of the use of language.[77]

Wittgenstein rejects the idea that there is primary data upon which all else depends such as Russell's 'ultimate furniture of the world'.

In the *Investigations* Wittgenstein clears his thinking from the bits of realism found in the *Tractatus*, where language and logic are independent of human life. Now he shows that knowledge and certainty are found within our lives and do not rely on external strictures (e.g. simple object, innate ideas, perceptual qualities, God). Language and the world do not link by means of independent elementary propositions, which are either true or false; rather, propositions are internally related and logic is based in language use, it is not that which underlies language. Wittgenstein notes:

> In reflecting on language and meaning we can easily get into a position where we think that in philosophy we are not talking of words and sentences in a quite common-or-garden sense, but in a subliminated and abstract sense – As if a particular proposition wasn't really the thing that some person utters, but an ideal entity (the 'class of all synonymous sentences' or the like). But is the chess knight that the rules of chess deal with such an ideal and abstract entity too? (We are not justified in having any more scruples about our language than the chess player has about chess, namely none.)[78]

The close relationship between language and life, in contrast to the realist and idealist, is evident in Wittgenstein's remark, 'to imagine a language means to imagine a form of life'.[79] The meaning of a word is not an object of logical analysis or experience, nor is it a mental process of ideas; rather, the meaning is the use of the word as applied in everyday life.

Consequently, exactness is not dependent on metaphysical foundations, it is found in our everyday lives and conversations that show what is ruled out of our everyday language, not by logic, but by the discourse itself (or if you prefer the logic of discourse). For example, we ask for five red apples and the shopkeeper gives us five red apples.[80] Wittgenstein says:

> Now think of the following use of language: I send someone shopping. I give him a slip marked 'five red apples'. He takes the slip to the shopkeeper, who opens

the drawer marked 'apples'; then he looks up the word 'red' in a table and finds a colour sample opposite; then he says the series of cardinal numbers – I assume that he knows them by heart – up to the word 'five' and for each number he takes an apple of the same colour as the sample out of the drawer – It is in this and similar ways that one operates with words – 'but how does he know where and how he is to look up the word "red" and what is he to do with the word "five"?' – no such thing was in question here, only how the word 'five' is used.[81]

If we focus on external foundations to gain exactness, we actually trade exactness for metaphysical theories.

Wittgenstein shows how, in his view, Augustine falls into the above confusion of not paying attention to the application of language and thereby holds a confused conception of language and meaning, that is, he wrongly views language as a system of signs which names objects in abstraction from application. Augustine notes:

> When they (my elders) named some object, and accordingly moved towards something, I saw this and I grasped that the thing was called by the sound they uttered when they meant to point it out. Their intention was shown by their bodily movements, as it were the natural language of all peoples: the expression of the face, and the tone of voice which expresses our state of mind in seeking, having, rejecting, or avoiding something. Thus, as I heard words repeatedly used in their proper places in various sentences, I gradually learnt to understand what objects they signified; and after I had trained my mouth to form these signs, I used them to express my own desires.[82]

Augustine's description of learning a language, according to Wittgenstein, is confused because it is tied to ostensive definition: 'The individual words in language name objects – sentences are combinations of such names – In this picture of language we find the roots of the following idea: Every word has a meaning. This meaning is correlated with the word. It is the object for which it stands.'[83] That this ostensive understanding of meaning does not work (in all cases) is demonstrated by the example of pointing to a knight on a chess board, in which case we may think the name knight refers to something that looks like a horse's head, but be completely unaware of how it is used in the game of chess. Moreover, what about words that are not names but have meaning, such as the exclamation 'Ow!' which cannot be understood through a name–object relation.[84]

Augustine's theory, according to Wittgenstein, not only simplifies language into names and objects, which erroneously assumes that the purpose of language is simply the name–object relation, but also implies that the subject has an innate language prior to learning a language. It assumes the agent already has a grasp of language, an innate language, that 'describes the learning of human language as if the child came into a strange country; and did not understand the language of the country; that is, as if it already had a language, only not this one'.[85] We can find the devaluation of the everyday use of language as the mode of meaning in Noam Chomsky and Jerry Fodor, both of whom posit an external foundation for language. Chomsky points to an innate inner reason or ability that enables language, as if we are hardwired for language and then simply place the word into the right spot. He writes: 'As a precondition for language learning, he must posses, first, a linguistic theory that specifies the form of the grammar of a possible human language, and, second, a strategy for selecting a grammar of the appropriate form that is compatible with the primary linguistic data.'[86] The logical conclusion of Chomsky's theory is noted and endorsed by Fodor; namely, 'one cannot learn that P falls under R unless one has a language in which P and R can be represented. So one cannot learn a language unless one has a language.'[87] Even if Wittgenstein admits that not all cases are a matter of learning words through use, it is nonetheless clear that he does not endorse an innate or instinctual language.[88]

Wittgenstein notes that when we try to explain how we learn a word such as 'book', we often forget the application and 'keep steering towards the idea of the private ostensive definition'.[89] This is why Wittgenstein's rejection of Augustine's ostensive definition is also a rejection of Descartes' solitary observer of the world. In contrast to ostensive definitions, Wittgenstein notes, we 'could not apply any rules to a *private* transition from what is seen to words. Here the rules really would hang in the air; for the institution of their use is lacking.'[90] In other words, we understand words by referring to something, so if language were abstracted from our everyday lives it would make no difference what is said, so nothing is understood. Hence, in contrast to private ostensive definitions, Wittgenstein remarks: 'How do I know this colour is red? – It would be an answer to say: I have learnt English.'[91] Learning English is an activity, it is not a recollection of innate knowledge or frameworks, nor is it simply a theory. There is no need for a metaphysical theory or underlying logical syntax; instead, 'the meaning of a word is a kind of employment of it. For it is what we learn when the word is incorporated into our language.'[92] Through the example of Augustine and learning language, Wittgenstein moves us away from erroneous conceptions of the solitary individual making links between the mind and the external world.

In the *Investigations* Wittgenstein uses his description of language to tie it to human activities (life), not upon formal unity or private observations. He gives up the idea that there is a general structure of language, and he moves from the temptation of linguistic realism in a Platonic form to the 'rough ground'. Wittgenstein says, 'the term "language-*game*" is meant to bring into prominence the fact that the speaking of a language is part of an activity of a form of life.'[93] Moreover, 'How should we get into conflict with the truth, if our footrules were made of very soft rubber instead of wood and steel? – "Well, we shouldn't get to know the correct measurement of the table." – You mean: we should not get, or could not be sure of getting, *that* measurement which we get with our rigid rulers.'[94] Additionally,

> the rules of grammar are arbitrary in the same sense as the choice of a unit of measurement. But that means no more than that the choice is independent of the length of the objects to be measured and that the choice of one unit is not 'true' and another 'false' in the way that a statement of length is true of false.[95]

Wittgenstein is emphasizing that the standard for correct or incorrect measuring is not an external measure, such as Platonic Forms or truths, but is a practical convention of our language-games.

Wittgenstein notes:

> I once wrote 'A proposition is like a ruler laid against reality.' Only the outermost graduating marks touch the object to be measured. I would now rather say: a *system* of propositions is laid against reality like a ruler. What I mean is this: when I lay a ruler against a spatial object, I lay all the graduating lines against it at the same time. It is not individual graduating lines that are laid against it, but the whole scale.[96]

There is no one measure of language that determines language. Instead, there is the entire system of language before us. Consequently, language is not based on an atomistic connection to the independent elementary proposition, which is either true or false. Instead, language is a network of internal relations between propositions that reflect the logic of language through everyday applications and human convention. Wittgenstein says, 'when philosophers use a word – "knowledge," "being" . . . and try to grasp the essence of the thing, one must always ask oneself: is the word ever actually used in this way in the language-game which is its original home? – What we do is to bring words back from their metaphysical to their everyday use.'[97] If we are unfamiliar with the terrain, the right action is not to theorize about the terrain, but to become familiar with the terrain, the rough ground of language use. Wittgenstein notes, 'philosophy simply puts everything before us, and neither explains nor deduces anything.'[98]

The language-games are not representing the formal unity of the *one* game, which would relapse into his old ways of thinking. Instead, the language-games are like many strands of a rope, not one rope.[99] Moreover, 'Our language can be seen as an ancient city: a maze of little streets and squares, of old and new houses, and of houses with additions from various periods; and this surrounded by a multitude of new boroughs with straight regular streets and uniform houses.'[100] Language works in the multiple paths of life, not an independent logical syntax.

If Wittgenstein emphasizes language-games and not a predetermined, independent and external foundation, then does it follow that he is an idealist? The answer is no. However, Bernard Williams wrongly thinks that Wittgenstein is an idealist, and it is not an uncommon assumption (largely because most philosophers and theologians usually regard themselves to be realists, and it is therefore thought that Wittgenstein's apparent rejection of realism must lead him to idealism). Williams notes:

> The way Wittgenstein conceives of this relation makes what its speakers call reality relative to and dependent on their language. He thus denies the existence, indeed, the very possibility of a reality outside the language a people speak and live with – that is a reality independent of that language. He rejects, that is, an absolute conception of reality as unintelligible. Consequently the objects that constitute what is ultimately real are denied an existence independent of the speakers of the language.[101]

The linguistic idealist denies that there is anything independent of language; instead, what we regard as reality is dependent on our language, that is, reality mirrors our language. It should be clear that this is the inverse of the *Tractatus*, where language mirrors the logical structure of the world. Linguistic idealism seems to leave language in an arbitrary position, with no anchor – which is exactly what the realist fears.

Is reality simply a human creation? It is clearly problematic to regard reality as a product of minds and language. What existed before humans and their ideas and language created anything? Note, however, that if reality is dependent on language, then the idealist may resort to appealing to a timeless foundation or language, such as the Berkeleyan God, in order to evade the criticism that there could obviously not be a reality prior to human beings creating it. By positing a God, it is then possible to make sense of prehistoric objects that are independent of human language and creation, but are internal to, and dependent upon, God's language. This is, however, realism in disguise. Idealism in this form, like realism, keeps an external and metaphysical foundation to which language must conform.

In any case, Wittgenstein's later work shows that he is not a realist and he is not an idealist. Wittgenstein never says that language use creates reality. Reality is larger, in a sense, than language. The whole, 'the natural history of human beings',[102] places us in a physical world where our traditions and customs play a role in the development of language. Yet at the same time, our grasp of that history, tradition and custom is mediated by language. Wittgenstein sees the question coming, so he notes, ' "So are you saying that human agreement decides what is true and what is false?" – It is what human beings say that is true and false; and they agree in the language they use. That is not agreement in opinions but in the form of life.'[103] We are not passive recipients (against realism), nor do we impose whatever we like on data (against idealism). This is similar to Wittgenstein's understanding of mathematics, where he rejects the realist idea that numbers mirror reality, and he rejects the formalist view that numbers are merely marks we play with; instead, it is in application that numbers become mathematics.[104] In contrast to Descartes' and Locke's dichotomy between language and reality, and ideas and reality, and in contrast to Berkeley's melding of these categories, the *Investigations* show that language and life are a whole and neither language nor life has priority over the other.

On Certainty

By the time of *On Certainty* Wittgenstein clearly continues the move away from the idea that the intelligibility of language depends on some metaphysical foundation, and that there is a general form of the proposition and a general structure of language. Once again, he is not trying to convince the sceptic that there are irrefutable propositions based on one foundational proposition (which would once again be realism); rather, he says that the sceptic's doubts are nonsense – he does not grant their metaphysical polemics a hearing. Wittgenstein is not searching for an epistemological relation that gives certitude to our knowledge or belief.

Wittgenstein says:

'An empirical proposition can be tested' (we say). But how?
And through what? What *counts* as its test? – 'But is this
an adequate test? And, if so, must it not be recognizable as
such in logic?' As if giving grounds did not come to an end
sometimes. But the end is not an ungrounded proposition:
it is an ungrounded way of acting.[105]

He notes the central role of acting, in contrast to pure thinking: 'Giving grounds, however justifying the evidence, comes
to an end; – but the end is not certain propositions striking us
immediately as true, i.e. it is not a kind of *seeing* on our part; it
is our *acting* which lies at the bottom of the language-game.'[106]
In other words, to say you know that there is a tree in your yard
is nothing more than reacting and acting in a certain way, to sit
under it, walk around it, prune it, and this certainty is based in
action instead of a rational decision. For example, 'Children do
not learn that books exist, that armchairs exist, etc., etc., – they
learn to fetch books, sit in arm chairs, etc., etc.,'[107] There is no
underlying logic here, 'it is part of the grammar of the word
"chair" that this is what we call "to sit in a chair"'.[108]

Moreover, in *On Certainty* we read,

[the child] doesn't learn *at all* that that mountain has
existed for a long time: that is, the question whether it
is so doesn't even arise. It swallows this consequence
down, so to speak, together with *what* it learns. The child
learns to believe a host of things. That is, it learns to act
according to these beliefs. Bit by bit there forms a system
of what is believed, and in that system some things stand
unshakeably fast and some are more or less liable to shift.
What stands fast does so, not because it is intrinsically
obvious or convincing; it is rather held fast by what lies
around it.'[109]

We do not *know* these things, we *live* them.

Wittgenstein notes, 'You must bear in mind that the
language-game is so to say something unpredictable. I mean: it

is not based on grounds. It is not reasonable (or unreasonable). It is there – like our life.'[110] Consequently, he rejects realism and epistemology when he says in *On Certainty*, 'why should the language-game rest on some kind of knowledge.'[111] The point here is that propositions such as 'the earth exists' are not empirical or epistemological, and do not need justification, it is instead the given. That we know something is not dependent upon the solitary subjective thinker, or something going on in your head; rather, it is a matter of grasping what others have at hand as well in the form of life.

Our surroundings, our way of acting and reacting, is part of what Wittgenstein calls our 'world-picture'. He says, 'I did not get my picture of the world by satisfying myself of its correctness; nor do I have it because I am satisfied of its correctness. No: it is the inherited background against which I distinguish between true and false.'[112] In *On Certainty* Wittgenstein shows how the realist is in error when attempting to justify a particular proposition since the realist misses the entire context. In contrast to any one independent foundation that language rests on, he says, 'one might almost say that these foundation-walls are carried by the whole house.'[113] He shows that language is embedded in our lives and that they develop together without one taking precedence over the other. He does not intend to justify knowledge or find guaranteed propositions; instead, there is a need to see the place that knowledge has in our lives. Consequently, we do not start with a single independent proposition to be verified on its own to build a system; rather, we start with a network of propositions – 'philosophy is not laid down in sentences, but in language'.[114]

Wittgenstein says, 'Am I not getting closer and closer to saying that in the end logic cannot be described? You must look at the practice of language then you will see it.'[115] What he sees is that what we can and cannot say, as found in the *Tractatus* and based on underlying logical syntax, is not as important as what we do say. The latter does not require justification or epistemological verification, it is the given that is tied to our everyday practices through which logic is shown. This logic that is shown in practices makes it clear that when I am typing it is nonsense to ask, 'Are you typing?' How could I reply to such a question? Wittgenstein retains the idea that there is some general unity, as found in the *Tractatus*, but this unity is not that of a logical underlying syntax, it is life itself! He writes, 'All testing, all confirmation and disconfirmation of a hypothesis takes place already within a system. And this system is not a more or less arbitrary and doubtful point of departure for all our arguments: no, it belongs to the essence of what we call an argument. The system is not so much the point of departure, as the element in which arguments have their life.'[116] Consequently, logical form changes; formerly it was the underpinning of language, later it is that which is shown in language and practices. Thus, if there were a disagreement in 'world pictures', then this would be understood through differences in practices and language applications, not through evidence and arguments (which has clear implications for the discussion on ecumenical dialogue in Part III).

Language mediates our contact with a reality that is not reduced to language; however, that reality so mediated is not independent of language. In a sense, logic was previously outside language, but by *On Certainty* logic is in language and shown through language. Logic is not a hidden underlying structure and it cannot be explained in abstraction; likewise, God in Christian thought is not hidden and cannot be explained in abstraction. Instead, we see logic in the activities of words and we see God in the Word. Wittgenstein's shift in understanding logic is thereby analogical to the shift in God's relation to the world from the Old Testament to the New Testament. When this understanding is tied to Wittgenstein's remark to Drury – 'your religious ideas have always seemed to me more Greek than biblical. Whereas my thoughts are one hundred percent Hebraic'[117] – the result, I suggest, is that we can see how Wittgenstein's thought moves from holding some aspects of Platonic realism in the *Tractatus*, to a more worldly and concrete Hebraic point of view, and ultimately his conception of logic shows similarities with the Word revealed (which has clear implications for the discussion on Christology in Part III).

Wittgenstein shifts the discussion from one of separation – that we and logic are independently related to the world – and the resultant theories that try to tie back together what has been torn asunder, to a discussion that shows how we and logic are in the world. To think otherwise leads Wittgenstein to remark on the consequence, 'We have got on to slippery ice where there is no friction and so in a certain sense the conditions are ideal, but also, just because of that, we are unable to walk. We want to walk: so we need *friction*. Back to the rough ground!'[118] Indeed, Wittgenstein says, 'I might say: if a place I want to get to could only be reached by way of a ladder, I would give up trying to get there. For the place I really have to get to is a place I must already be now. Anything that I might reach by climbing a ladder does not interest me.'[119] In *On Certainty* he points out that there is no place to reach outside the language-game to secure knowledge, such as the Cartesian Archimedean point. Likewise, in theology, there is no place to reach outside of Christ to better understand God (this has clear implications for the discussion on the theology of the cross in Part III). The language-games and Christ are the heart of meaning and they show logic and God respectively.

Part III
Theology

Chapter 5

Wittgenstein and Theology

A discussion of Wittgenstein and theology is certain to generate criticism from many angles given the variants in interpreting Wittgenstein compounded by various theological points of view. My intent is not to show the only way that he can be applied to theology, but a way that might lead to further useful discussions. My method is not to show what Wittgenstein's personal beliefs are in particular, or to determine whether or not he is religious in general, but is to show how aspects of his philosophy correlate with aspects of theology. In particular, I intend to show that his conception of logic, language and our everyday lives in philosophy fits analogically with Chalcedonian Christology, and that these two aspects – philosophical and theological – are central to understanding the nature of theology.

Wittgensteinian fideism

A brief note on the so-called Wittgensteinian fideism is required, even though it is not central to my argument, since it is a misleading label that is often associated with Wittgenstein. This unhelpful label could easily hinder Wittgenstein's reception into theology since it replaces the insightful nature of his philosophy with a theory. Fideism itself goes back to the early church when the relationship between faith and reason was questioned. For example, the church father Tertullian (*c.* AD 160–230) notes: 'What indeed has Athens to do with Jerusalem?'[120] This infamous remark notes a distinction between reason and faith, and Athens and Jerusalem, respectively; and has fuelled endless debates to the present regarding the nature of this relationship.

Fideism is a term derived from the Latin word for faith (*fides*). The general idea is that faith is independent of, and perhaps opposed to, reason in matters of theology. This dynamic plays into the atheist philosopher Kai Nielson's perspective. He thinks that either universal reason applies to religion and faith or it does not. If not, then religion and faith are meaningless. He regards Wittgensteinians (e.g. D. Z. Phillips, Norman Malcolm, and Peter Winch in particular) as supporters of fideism and rejecters of reason in matters of religion, and since they use Wittgenstein's notion of language-games in their arguments, he concludes that this is a 'Wittgensteinian fideism'. [121] Indeed, Nielson coined this term and it has subsequently taken on a particularly virulent nature. Did Wittgenstein ever support fideism? No. Do the philosophers accused of Wittgensteinian fideism support fideism? No. Rather, an atheistic philosopher has coined a term that misrepresents Wittgenstein and those who follow his thought and, regrettably, it can lead to a misrepresentation of Wittgenstein's philosophy in its application to religion in general and theology in particular. Nielsen assumes that there is one universal discourse that we all agree upon. Consequently, we can also agree upon what does and does not fit rational discourse – we can agree upon what is and is not rational. In the case of religious beliefs, he suggests that Wittgensteinian fideism argues that only those who participate in a particular religious language-game understand those very religious beliefs, and since that language-game is not connected to any other part of life it follows that it cannot be criticized. We cannot use the one universal discourse of reason to critique religious beliefs since they reside outside of it.

Many wrongly believe that this is not only the consequence, but also the point of a Wittgensteinian approach to religious belief; namely, to set up a defence against any criticism that may be levelled against religious belief. However, does a Wittgensteinian point of view deliberately defend religious belief from all criticism, is religion logically removed from all other discourse and aspects of life? Wittgenstein argues against the theory that there is a unity to all language, and that there is some abstract thing that is common to all language. Nielson therefore assumes that when this is applied to religion the result is fideism. Although Nielson admits that Wittgenstein cannot be charged with Wittgensteinian fideism, he assumes that the

Wittgensteinians can be so charged and are guilty. The problem here is that Wittgenstein's philosophy does not offer the support to fideism that Nielson thinks it does. Therefore, not only are the Wittgensteinians innocent of the charge, Wittgenstein never supplied the motive in the first place. For Wittgenstein, the relation between language-games becomes clear through the realization that a particular language-game – although it is not part of the *one* game – necessarily connects with other language-games. He is not arguing for a complete discontinuity. He notes that there is 'a complicated network of similarities overlapping and criss-crossing'.[122] For example, worship is not simply an autonomous activity that has nothing to do with life and is consequently immune to any criticism you or I may have against it. Wittgenstein does not say anything goes, in contrast he notes, 'Religious faith and superstition are quite different. One of them results from *fear* and is a sort of false science. The other is a trusting.'[123] What if someone said, 'I believe that God exists, that God resides in the centre of the earth, and that I will visit God once I figure out how to dig a deep enough hole.' Would the Wittgensteinian say that this belief is beyond criticism? No, it is beyond meaning. The language-game of Christianity is tied directly to the language-games of death, birth, marriage, sin, etc., and we understand these contexts.

Is this a contradiction? Are the religious language-games both independent and dependent? The independence rests on the fact that there is no one game or unity that sustains language and determines it. The dependence rests on the fact that just as we cannot have a private language we cannot have a private language-game. Importantly, this dependence is not one of justification, epistemology or foundations, but our acting. Paul Holmer, who effectively uses Wittgenstein's philosophy, rightly notes that the emphasis on forms of life makes it seem 'as though fideism is more crucial than theology. So it is that followers of Wittgenstein and Wittgenstein himself are assumed to be of the mind that denies that there is a recognisable kind of knowledge of God and that therefore theology is not truly cognitive, objective, and rational'.[124] Moreover, Holmer notes, 'theology is not knowledge of God by analogy with physics and geology.'[125] However, Nielsen is not happy with the idea that his philosophy cannot criticize religious belief and that he cannot set out to show that religious propositions must be either true or false. Once again, this shows how Wittgenstein can be misread since it is thought there is only one form of reason, as if the scientific method applies to all of life, and all we need to do is have others repeat the experiment and then we can all clearly see that this or that belief is or is not justified.

What the Wittgensteinians are arguing against is the account Nielson would give of the connection between religion and human life, they are not arguing that there is *no* connection and therefore no criticism! There is a connection between religion and life. Religion is not completely cut off. Yet this is not a matter of epistemology, it is one of practice. To say that we can only understand what religious belief is by seeing the language-game in its form of life is not fideism, it is common sense. Try to understand music without music; try to understand sport without sport; try to understand religion without religion. Granted, analogies and cross references can be made that are outside music, sport and religion, but you must understand what music, sport and religion are in the first place before you can make any comparison.

The above conception of Wittgensteinian fideism has worked its way into theology. For example, if we take Nielsen's misconception and place it into theology the result may be the following: since Wittgenstein regards religion as an entirely independent language-game and free from criticism, it then follows that religion is removed from its ontological foundations.[126] Without this ontological foundation, belief is stripped of its ontological truth. This follows the same reasoning as Nielson but inverts the problematic conclusion – Wittgenstein wrongly opens belief to rejection.

In contrast to these misconceptions of Wittgenstein's philosophy, it is important to see that he, and those following him, do not hold to a general unity of language comparable to a logical system (as in the *Tractatus*) or some other metaphysical Archimedean point, but direct us to the interconnectedness of language-games in our forms of life. These forms of life do not represent a formal unity that enforces what must be said (can and cannot say); instead, they show what we do say. A Wittgensteinian view does not protect what religion says from criticism; it shows the nature of what is said. Religion cannot be rejected or justified by external standards, and at the same time, religion is not isolated from all externalities by setting up its own little realm of standards.

The problem with Wittgensteinian fideism is that it turns the discussion into polemics and away from Wittgenstein's insights. The following discussion is meant to bring forth a Wittgensteinian understanding of the nature of religious belief rather than argue for or against religious belief.

Towards a Wittgensteinian view

Wittgenstein's philosophy begins with logic underlying language and, in a sense, hidden, but ends by showing that logic is revealed in language. Once again, this is comparable to the shift from the Old Testament, where God was in a sense partially hidden (Moses only sees the backside of God) to the New Testament where God is revealed. This analogy can be further explored though a discussion of Christology. The fundamental question of Christology is the relation between the divine and human, and this aspect can be paralleled to Wittgenstein's conception of the relation between logic and language.

Additionally, in the previous section the question was also, 'How do ideas relate to the external world?' In the case of Cartesianism, we saw that the individual perceiver is distanced from that which would provide meaning; namely, the world. This leads to questions concerning the relation between the mind and body and can result in dualism. In philosophy, the separation of one's mind from the world, and ideas from substance, leads to the complexity of trying to explain how they are related. To answer this question Locke essentially reinforces the distinction while Berkeley collapses the distinction. The relationship between logic–language and ideas–substance pairings, as discussed in the above section, now includes the divine–human pairing. Moreover, parallel arguments can be drawn between Locke–Nestorianism and Berkeley–Eutychianism.

Behind Locke and Berkeley resides Descartes, and behind Nestorius and Eutyches resides Plato. Despite the differences between Plato and Descartes, it is nonetheless interesting to briefly point out potential similarities between them in terms of their thought and in terms of their influence upon theology and philosophy. A comprehensive discussion of the similarities and differences between Plato and Descartes and their influence is clearly beyond the present discussion, but it is worthwhile to note.

Like Descartes, who begins his philosophical method by rejecting the senses, Plato seeks knowledge by means of reason. Plato tells us to turn away from the cave (our sensory experiences) towards the world of forms (reason). By turning away from the world of shadows and change to the Forms we discern that the rational mind is distinct and logically separable from the body and its senses. For instance, Plato notes:

> Then he will do this most perfectly who approaches the object with thought alone, without associating any sight with his thought, or dragging in any sense perception with his reasoning, but who, using pure thought alone, tries to track down reality pure and by itself, freeing himself as far as possible from the eyes and ears, and in a word from the whole body, because the body confuses the soul and does not allow it to acquire truth and wisdom whenever it associates with it.[127]

This separation of reason and the senses fundamentally separates the mind from the body. Wittgenstein notes of the expression, 'I am in pain' – but 'how can I go so far as to try to use language to get between pain and its expression?'[128] That is, I can try to separate sensation and expression only if I keep the metaphysical idea that language merely names objects. I can then treat my feelings as objects of private observation, in other words, I can escape the body.[129] It is this escape that Plato seems to endorse. The separation between the senses and reason enforces the separation between the mind and body.

There is clear similarity between Plato's and Descartes' devaluation of the senses and the physical world. Hobbes even notes: 'Plato and other ancient philosophers discussed this uncertainty in the objects of the senses . . . I am sorry that the author [Descartes], who is so outstanding in the field of original speculations, should publish this ancient material.'[130] Whether or not Descartes' meditations are a modern revisiting of Plato's cave analogy, in both Descartes and Plato there is a turning inward towards reason. The forms are, so to speak, beyond the heavens, but they are known inwardly. For Plato and Descartes the *a priori* and unchanging formal unity of reality that reason discerns is the foundation – for Descartes it is God, who is the anchor that makes his perceptions true; for Plato, the Good is that on which the plurality of Forms depend.

These conceptions of a transcendent and metaphysical foundation, in a theological context, yield an immutable and eternal God that is more of a Greek conception of God than a Judaeo-Christian conception. The Greek conception of God deals in abstractions, while the Judaeo-Christian conception of God is more concrete (and closer to Wittgenstein's philosophy). For example, the Christian conception of God is that the Word is made flesh. The Jewish conception of God is also concrete. For instance, Solomon Schechter remarks:

> Among the many strange statements by which the Jewish student is struck, when reading modern divinity works, there is none more puzzling to his mind than the assertion of the transcendentalism of the Rabbinic God. Sayings of a fantastic nature . . . epithets for God, such as Heaven or Supreme . . . or the Master of all Creation [are] Hellenistic phrases which crept into Jewish literature, but never received, in the mouth of a Rabbi, the significance which they had with an Alexandrine philosopher.[131]

Moreover, Abraham Heschel observes, 'Plato planted in the Western mind the consciousness of unseen, eternal ideas, of which the visible world is but a copy. The prophets placed in the Western mind the consciousness of an unseen, eternal God, of whose Will the visible world is a creation.'[132] The Judaeo-Christian conception of God is akin to Wittgenstein's conception of logic from the *Tractatus* to *On Certainty*. Although there are aspects of Platonic realism in the *Tractatus* whereby logic is an independent metaphysical foundation, logic is nonetheless part of the world and it determines the formation of language. The Later Wittgenstein, however, takes one more step away from the Greek conception and shows that logic is revealed in language. In a sense, we could say Wittgenstein embeds the Platonic Forms in the visible world. Theologically speaking this is like a turn from the unseen Greek Forms and symbolic world, to the Hebraic God working in the visible and non-symbolic world, culminating in the Christian revealed God.

I will argue in the following that Platonic and Cartesian thought open the fly bottle in philosophy and theology. In other words, they both at least indirectly foster theories that set a precedent on reason and metaphysics outside our physical and fleeting world, and this results in a problematic separation between the idea–substance and divine–human pairings. The subsequent heirs of this starting point can err on one of two sides, endorse a strict separation (Realism: Locke and Nestorianism) or collapse it (Idealism: Berkeley and Eutyches). The prevalent Western tradition of philosophy and a large section of theology typically follow these Platonic and Cartesian paths – whereas Wittgenstein does not, nor does Chalcedon.

For example, in the line of Zwingli and Calvin there is still some adherence to this Platonic path. Calvin says:

> The swiftness with which the human mind glances from heaven to earth, scans the secrets of nature, and, after it has embraced all ages, with intellect and memory digest each other in its proper order, and reads the future in the past, clearly demonstrates that there lurks in man a something separated from the body. We have an intellect by which we are able to conceive of the invisible God and angels – a thing of which the body is altogether incapable.[133]

Calvin is right; the body is 'altogether incapable'! However, is the mind capable of scanning the secrets of nature and conceiving of angles in abstraction? Unsurprisingly, Calvin thinks the soul is to be freed of the 'prison-house of the body', since 'men cleaving too much to the earth are dull of apprehension' and the soul is the 'nobler part'.[134] The point here is not that the soul is actually not noble; rather, the important point is that Calvin clearly regards the body as less noble. Since earthly musings are devalued, it is a natural consequence for Calvin to say, 'The knowledge of God has been naturally implanted in the human mind.'[135] Nietzsche has harsh words for this aspect of Plato's thought: 'I should prefer to describe the entire phenomenon "Plato" by the harsh term "higher swindle" or, if you prefer, "idealism", than by any other.'[136]

Moreover, as will be shown below, the Reformed tradition not only separates the mind from the world, but also the human nature from the divine nature in Christ. For example, given the great divide between the divine and the human it follows that the human attributes of Jesus cannot be communicated to the divine. This will be shown as central to a Reformed understanding of the sacrament of the Lord's Supper as well where, in contrast to the Catholic tradition, there is a similar separation of the physical from the divine. Given the emphasis on reason, and the chasm between the human/physical and the spiritual/divine, it is thought to be clearly unreasonable to assume that the divine is physically present in mere bread – it is only a symbol of a heavenly reality.

Wittgenstein writes in the Foreword of *Philosophical Remarks*:

This book is written for such men as are in sympathy with its spirit. This spirit is different from the one which informs the vast stream of European and American civilization in which all of us stand. That spirit expresses itself in an onwards movement, in building ever larger and more complicated structures; the other in striving after clarity and perspicuity in no manner what structure. The first tries to grasp the world by way of its periphery – in its variety; the second at its centre – its essence. And so the first adds one construction to another, moving on and up, as it were, from one stage to the next, while the other remains where it is and what it tries to grasp is always the same.[137]

I suggest that Wittgenstein's philosophy is written in a spirit that is opposed to the typical Greek tradition, and I also suggest that Chalcedon is likewise opposed to the Greek tradition. Wittgenstein's philosophy moves away from the prevalent Western tradition of philosophy and analogically towards Jewish thought and finally Christian thought.

Once again, this does not mean that he became a Christian; indeed, I am not implying anything about his personal beliefs or preferences. Rather, his thought is analogical to theology – but not any theology. Certainly not reformed theology, but it is clearly comparable to the Chalcedonian Christology and its natural consequences. Neither Wittgenstein in philosophy nor Chalcedon in theology constructs further theories or explanations. Instead, as Wittgenstein notes, 'Our illness is this, to want to explain.'[138] Consequently, 'philosophy isn't anything except philosophical problems'.[139] Once again, the best way to show the nature of Wittgenstein's philosophy is to show how it deals with illness through the *via negativa*.

Christology: Nestorian and Eutychian

Christology is the study of Christ, and in particular the relation between the human and divine natures. Unsurprisingly, this debate takes various forms based on the obvious difference between the divine and human natures. For example, Nestorius was the patriarch of Constantinople in 428 and was a driving force of Christological discussions. In particular, he argued for a clear separation between the divine and human natures in Christ, and some have drawn the conclusion that it was such a strict separation that he ended up with two Christs, one with the divine nature and one with the human nature. Whether or not this is an accurate and fair depiction of his thought is beyond this discussion, yet it is important to note that Nestorius may not have held the extreme view attributed to him by his opponents. Instead of arguing for the accurate interpretation of Nestorius the point here is to note the school of thought that follows him by name; namely, Nestorianism.

Nestorius was cautious of the Alexandrian's use of the term *Theotokos* (God bearer) since he thought that it implied a confusion of the divine with the human. He considered it inconceivable that the divine could actually be born since being born is a human characteristic. For instance, Nestorius writes:

> It is not possible that the unmade (should become) made and the eternal temporary and the temporary eternal and that the created (should become) uncreated by nature; that that which is uncreated and which has not come into being and is eternal should thereby become made and temporary, as if it became part of a nature made and temporary; nor that there should come forth a nature unmade and eternal from nature made and temporary to become an *ousia* [substance] unmade and eternal; for such things are not possible nor conceivable.[140]

This links with Platonic philosophical views in the sense that God is unchanging, impassable, eternal, etc., only humans change, are passable and mortal. In agreement with this view, Theodore of Mopsuestia (d. 428) writes:

> It is well known that the one who is eternal, and the one whose existence came into being later, are separated from each other, and the gulf between them unbridgeable. . . . It is not possible to limit and define the chasm that exists between the one who is from eternity and the one who began to exist at a time when he was not. What possible resemblance and relation can exist between two beings so widely separated from each other.[141]

Nestorianism continues this separation of two clearly distinct natures that cannot be confused; therefore, because the two natures are separated in spite of the incarnation, it then follows that there are two independent and complete individuals. Thus, the second person of the trinity took the human nature as a form to work through and through whom there was a unity of purpose; while each entity – the divine and the human – remained independent. For instance, if there is a close union with the flesh and the flesh receives sense impressions, then how can there be immutability and impassability? Rather than admitting to one individual with human and divine natures that has such

sensations, Nestorianism instead argues that in Christ the individual who is a man suffers and the individual who is divine
performs divine operations such as miracles, each by means of
their own nature and attributes. The divine nature does not suffer; however, Christ does suffer. Therefore, we can either say
God suffers, or we split Christ into two. Nestorianism agrees
with the latter and thereby sacrificed the unity of Christ and
spoke of Mary as the Christ bearer (*Christotokos*) rather than God
bearer (*Theotokos*). Mary gave birth to the human who did not
have the divine nature; instead, the divine nature of the second
person of the trinity became united to the human that was born.
Consequently, Mary did not give birth to God and God does
not suffer.

Obviously, Nestorianism did not allow the full communication of attributes (*idiomata*) from the human nature to the
divine which is a natural consequence of regarding the divine as
impassable, unchanging, immortal, etc.; and that the finite is not
capable of the infinite. Nonetheless, Nestorianism agrees that
there is a union, but instead of a hypostatic (personal) union,
it is a moral union. That is, the human Christ fulfils the moral
will of the divine Christ. Thus, the problem of a physical unity
is eased by saying that it is a moral and pragmatic unity instead.
At best, Nestorianism held a weak understanding of the union
in one Christ; at worst, it ended with two Christs.

Nestorianism wants to protect the independence of God to
avoid confusing the divine and human natures, and Locke wants
to protect the independent nature of matter to avoid confusing
ideas and substance. In both cases the human nature and substance are taken seriously; however, both theories end up with
difficulties because they begin with a strict separation between
the divine–human and ideas–substance, respectively. In other
words, the problem of two Christs, the human and the divine,
in Nestorianism is similar to the problem of two qualities, primary and secondary, in Locke's theory. Locke does not allow
substance (particularly the primary quality) to reach the mind
since it is not perceivable, just as Nestorianism does not allow
the divine to substantially contact the human because it sur-
passes humanity. The consequence in both of these cases is an
unknown metaphysical foundation. Locke has the 'I know not

what' substance and Nestorianism ends up with a hidden God, or at least one that is not fully revealed. In both cases, we have at best secondary qualities that represent these unknown and hidden foundations.

I suggest that much of the protestant tradition is in accord with this strict separation between the divine and the human and rejects the full communication of attributes on rational grounds: including the Reformed axiom: *finitum non est capax infiniti* (the finite is not capable of the infinite). Moreover, the Reformed tradition, following Zwingli, uses terms such as *alloeosis* (mutual exchange) to protect the divine (utter transcendence) from the human and, in particular, to protect the divine from suffering. The *alloeosis* is a rhetorical figure of speech that allows one to speak of Christ's human nature but actually refer to his divine nature. The implications of this aspect of the Reformed tradition, that is, the denial of the communication of attributes in Christology, carries into the Lord's Supper whereby the finite bread cannot contain the divine physically and at best is a symbol pointing to a spiritual reality.

This continues the separation seen in the Nestorian divide between the divine and human natures, and is analogical to Locke's divide between substance and ideas. In each of these cases, there are external foundations that determine meaning, even though each of these foundations is completely beyond our grasp and remain ultimately unknown. The Nestorian God remains an abstraction and Locke's substance remains an abstract unknown something. In both cases, what we have at best are symbols and representations – as is found in Greek thought.

There is an alternative Christology that keeps similar suppositions as the Nestorian view, but comes to an opposite conclusion. Eutyches (*c.* 448) was the archimandrite of a cloister in Constantinople and he inspired the school of thought known as Eutychianism. Once again, as is the case for Nestorius, I am not arguing for the accurate interpretation of Eutyches; rather, the point lies in the Eutychian school of thought that takes his name.

The concern for the unity of the divine influences the Eutychian view just as it influenced the Nestorian view. In both cases, the incarnation is too perplexing and incongruous; the divine must be 'protected' from the human. However, in contrast to Nestorianism, the thought of two Christs or two natures was rejected as a blatant confusion. Consequently, the concern for unity went to the opposite extreme. Instead of protecting the divine from the human through separation, the divine engulfs the human completely. The Eutychian view argues that before the union there were two natures, but after the union there was one.

Given that Eutychianism argues that Christ has one nature, it is natural to ask, 'Is it the case that the one nature is derived from the divine and human natures, or is one nature essentially annihilated?' For Eutychianism, the stronger nature prevails over the weaker nature. Therefore, it is the case that 'the Godhead remains and that the manhood was absorbed by it;' moreover, it is 'like the sea receiving a drop of honey, for straightaway the drop, as it mixes with the sea's water, vanishes.'[142] Even if it is argued that the human nature is not entirely annihilated, it is nonetheless transmuted into the divine. Moreover, the body of Christ is so deified that it is no longer consubstantial with us. Whereas the Nestorian view held that the human nature of Christ was like us, the Eutychian view is that Christ's one nature is not really human. This view consequently holds that there is not simply an abstract moral or pragmatic union between the human nature's operation and the divine nature's will, as is found in Nestorianism, but a substantial union of oneness.

In a sense, Eutychianism agreed with Nestorianism that if there are two natures in a union then there are logically two individuals, but Eutychianism rejects the possibility of two individuals and therefore concludes that there is a substantial union of only one nature. As Berkeley drew out the logical conclusion of Locke's philosophy, perhaps Eutychianism draws out the logical conclusion of Nestorianism. Yet there is a question lurking behind the Eutychian conception of union. If there is one individual and one nature, then what does the union consist of? In a sense, it would be accurate to say there is no union if there are not two natures to make a union. In the Eutychian tradition, the divine relationship to the human is better represented as annihilation than a union. The human nature was completely absorbed by the divine and it was no longer possible to speak of the human and divine natures separately.

Eutyches tried to resolve the problem of Nestorianism separating the divine and human natures, just as Berkeley tried to resolve the problem of Locke separating ideas and substance. The Eutychian answer is to transmute the human nature into the divine nature, just as Berkeley essentially transmutes matter into ideas. In other words, Eutychianism emphasizes the unity and divinity of Christ and thereby rejects the problematic two individuals and natures and collapses the human into the divine; Berkeley emphasizes the precedent of ideas and thereby rejects the problematic distinction between ideas and substance and collapses substance into ideas. The mediation of a physical world or nature is rejected in favour of an immediate union that logically amounts to no union. In both cases, theological and philosophical, the material and physical world is rejected in favour of something (or nothing) ethereal.

What about the communication of attributes? In the case of Nestorianism, the full communication of attributes is rejected. In the case of Eutychianism, many regard the problem to be that the human attributes are not communicated to the divine. However, from the above points, it should be clear that a discussion of the communication of attributes is mute. The significant point is not that Eutychianism does not allow the full communication of attributes; rather, the significant point is that it does not allow a human nature. Consequently, what exactly would a communication of attributes entail? There is only one nature, so where is there room for communication? Likewise, questions concerning how our ideas relate to substance are mute in Berkeley's world. Berkeley emphasizes ideas over the reality of an external physical world, and Eutychianism emphasizes the divine over the reality of a human being incarnated.

For Descartes, Locke and Berkeley, what we really have is our ideas while the physical world is either inferred and somewhat unknown or outright rejected. For Platonic thought, Nestorianism and Eutychianism, what is certain is a divine unity, while human participation and communication with the divine is turned into a weak abstract union (symbolic union) or is outright rejected.

Wittgenstein and Chalcedon

The Council of Ephesus (431) dealt with the Nestorian error of positing a Christ with two centres of personality by clearly arguing that the one Christ is not divided into two Christs, and the union is not an abstract agreement in morals or one of authority. Rather, there is a substantial physical unity. The Council of Chalcedon (451) continues this description of Christ and includes statements against Eutyches position that there is one Christ with one nature since the church confessed that the one Christ has two natures. To this end, the Bishops at Chalcedon agreed that:

> Following the holy Fathers, we with one voice confess our Lord Jesus Christ to be one and the same Son, perfect in divinity and humanity, truly God and truly human, consisting of a rational soul and a body, being of one substance with the Father in relation to his divinity, and being of one substance with us in relation to his humanity, and is like us in all things apart from sin (Hebrews 4.15). He was begotten of the Father before time in relation to his divinity, and in these recent days, was from the Virgin Mary, the *Theotokos*, for us and for our salvation. In relation to the humanity, he is one and the same Christ, the Son, the Lord, the Only-begotten, who is to be acknowledged in two natures, without confusion, without change, without division, and without separation. This distinction of natures is in no way abolished on account of this union, but rather the characteristic property of each nature is preserved, and concurring into one Person and one subsistence, not as if Christ were parted or divided into two persons, for he remains one and the same Son and Only-begotten God, Word, Lord, Jesus Christ; even as the Prophets from the beginning spoke concerning him, and our Lord Jesus Christ instructed us, and the Creed of the Fathers was handed down to us.[143]

This Chalcedonian Christology was put into creedal formulation in the Athanasian creed between the fifth and sixth centuries:

against Eutychianism Jesus is 'perfect God and perfect man' and this is so 'not by confusion of substance but by unity of person' and, against Nestorianism, 'although Jesus is God and man, he is not two Christ's but one Christ.' Christ is one person with two distinct natures; the divine nature has the attributes of God and the human nature has the attributes and limitations of humans. However, because of the personal union each nature operates through the other in the one person Christ.

To accept Chalcedon is to accept that Christ has a human nature and a divine nature. Yet the problematic relationship between the human and divine natures remained a point of debate. For example, given that the divine nature in the abstract does not suffer can we nonetheless say the divine suffers in light of the communication of attributes? If we say Jesus made a table with four legs and this Jesus is the Son of God in one person, then there would be agreement. However, if we say God made a table with four legs, then disagreement follows since making a table is the attribute of the human nature, not the divine nature. Likewise, if we say God was crucified and suffered, the response would be that being crucified and suffering is the attribute of the human nature, not the divine nature. However, with a full communication of attributes we can say Christ has died and we can thereby also say God has died – but importantly not God isolated, rather as united with Christ. God suffers because of the substantial union of the divine and human natures in one person Christ. Luther, for example, follows the Chalcedon view that what is attributed to one nature is attributed to the whole person:

> since the divinity and humanity are one person in Christ, the Scriptures ascribe to the divinity, because of this personal union, all that happens to humanity, and vice versa. . . . Just as we say: the king's son is wounded – when actually only his leg is wounded; Solomon is wise – though only his soul is wise; Absalom is handsome – though only his body is handsome; . . . For since the body and soul are one person, everything that pertains to the body or soul, yes, to the last member of the body, is correctly and properly ascribed to the whole person.[144]

God dies and suffers because there is one person – Christ – who has the attributes of both natures.

In contrast, Zwingli's rhetorical *alloeosis* weakens the communication of attributes and separates the divine nature from the human Jesus. Zwingli holds a nominal relation between the divine and human natures and thereby appears to support the Nestorian position. He notes, 'it was only the man who felt the pangs of suffering, and not God, for God is invisible, and therefore is not subject to any pain, that is, suffering or passion.'[145] Once again, we can see a Platonic type conception of God that creates a strict separation between the divine and the human. Granted, there is a great divide between the divine and the human; however, that is exactly why the incarnation is so extraordinary, it would not be extraordinary if it were not a substantial union. Luther is against such abstract rationalism:

> If I speak rightly saying that the divinity does not suffer,
> the humanity does not create, then I speak of something
> in the abstract and of a divinity that is separated. But one
> must not do that. Abstract concepts should not be cut
> loose, or our faith will become false. But one believes in
> a concrete sense (*in concreteo*) saying that this man is God,
> etc. Then the properties are attributed.[146]

Luther sees God as Christ in the concrete, not bound by Platonic categories and thereby transcending suffering. God is incarnated and is known in the flesh and blood rather than through abstract rationalizations. Therefore, the *alloeosis* is rejected.

Likewise, by comparison, the *alloeosis* is rejected analogically in Wittgenstein's later thought since logic is revealed in language. Wittgenstein's early work held elements of the *alloeosis* since logic determined language, which in turn did not communicate anything to logic. However, Wittgenstein came to see that logic is shown in language, which is not a symbol of logic, but is where logic substantially resides. To search for logic outside of language is an error; for Chalcedon, to search for God outside of Christ is an error. Wittgenstein's shift from epistemology to logic, from an underlying logical form to logic shown in the application of language, is analogical to the communication of attributes and incarnation. Christ mediates God and language mediates logic, without either one taking precedent – in contrast to Nestorian–Locke and Eutychian–Berkeley.

I admit that it is a stretch, but it is interesting to note, once again, that Wittgenstein says, 'When I think of the Jewish Bible, the Old Testament on its own, I feel like saying: the head is (still) missing from this body. These problems have not been solved. These hopes have not been fulfilled.'[147] The Old Testament observes, 'For my thoughts are not your thoughts, neither are your ways my ways says the Lord. For as the heavens are higher than earth so are my ways higher than your ways, and my thoughts than your thoughts.'[148] This is comparable to the *Tractatus* where the metaphysical underlying logical syntax is outside human everyday life, while the New Testament and the *Investigations* bring God and logic into human life, respectively. Wittgenstein's problems in logic had not been worked out until the *Investigations* and *On Certainty*, in particular, where a once hidden logic is shown; and in the case of Christianity, a once hidden God is shown. This may shed light of the continual debate about the continuity or lack of continuity in Wittgenstein's thought. It is clear that we cannot say the *Tractatus* is identical to the *Investigations*, Wittgenstein says 'It suddenly seemed to me that I should publish those old thoughts and the new ones together: that the latter could be seen in the right light only by contrast with and against the background of my old way of thinking.'[149] The old and New Testaments, the old and new thoughts, bear some analogy.

Interestingly, there may be dissatisfaction with Chalcedon and Wittgenstein since neither provides a comprehensive metaphysical theory; instead, they stop further explanations. As Wittgenstein notes, 'all that philosophy can do is destroy idols;' and importantly, 'that means not creating a new one'.[150] Chalcedon and Wittgenstein's philosophy do not represent advancements or progress in theories, nor do they represent apologetics for one side of polemical argument; rather, they take us back out of the fly bottle that holds the human made idols. Wittgenstein says, 'don't think, but look!'[151] We need to look to words and practices in the form of life to see logic and God. Whereas the theories interested in securing the transcendence of the divine say 'Don't look, think!'

Chapter 6

Wittgenstein and the Theologian

Wittgenstein is not offering a new theory, he is instead showing the confusion of theories as we found through Descartes, Locke and Berkeley, and comparatively through Platonic thought, Nestorianism and Eutychianism. How does this apply to theology today? Generalizations are always dangerous; nonetheless, it is helpful to make a demarcation between those who stay within (in various ways) the confines of the above theories in contrast to those who reject the pull of these arguments and side with Wittgenstein's and Chalcedon's limit of explanation. The former will be grouped under the umbrella of the theology (philosophy) of glory, while the latter will be grouped under what can be called the theology (philosophy) of the cross. It may be more fitting – and inclusive to Wittgenstein – to use the titles 'theology and philosophy of ladders' and the 'theology and philosophy of the rough ground', but in keeping with the theological nomenclature I will use the former title that Luther introduces.

In general, the theology of glory turns to the hidden and abstract God, while the theology of the cross turns to the revealed God – Christ crucified. In other words, the theology of glory seeks unmediated knowledge of the transcendent God by means of reason, while the theology of the cross seeks mediated knowledge of God by means of Christ. Roughly put, the Locke–Nestorian and Berkeley–Eutychian arguments, among others, analogically fit the way of glory, while Wittgenstein and Chalcedon analogically fit the way of the cross.

There is, of course, a grey area between these broad categories, and a great diversity within each category. Moreover, it is obviously impossible to definitively demarcate the factions within Christendom, as if all Liberal theologians think this way, and all post-Liberal theologians think that way. Or all Catholics think this way, and all Evangelicals think that way. The endless array of -ism's also makes it an exceedingly complicated task to spell out each one in detail. Nonetheless, there is a general distinction between those who tend to climb ladders to abstractions and those who prefer to remain on the rough ground.

The theology of glory

The above questions and theories of Locke and Berkeley are, in part, a result of questions that began with Descartes. Once the space between the observer and the world was opened Locke and Berkeley tried to mend it. What occurred in philosophy also occurred in theology, where, for example, Greek apologetics began to inform theology. The Alexandrians were apt apologists, as were some Jewish thinkers in the area such as Philo, who used Greek philosophy for their arguments. The danger, of course, was that Greek philosophy then directed the questions and, consequently, the answers as well. I suggest that those who are more closely associated with the tradition of Platonic and Cartesian thought can be included in the category of the theology of glory.

Once God is thought of in terms of Greek thought (e.g. the immutable truth above us), then it is not a large step to devaluing the significance of the earth, religious practices and the Word made flesh as means to show us God. The theology of glory posits a powerful and immutable God beyond our world that takes precedence over the symbols in the world. This is why there is often a greater interest in Wittgenstein's *Tractatus* and his early thoughts on silence and the mystical from this perspective; they are more closely associated with a Greek and Nestorian viewpoint of an independent metaphysical foundation. Phillip Shields, for example, writes, 'Wittgenstein's characterization of God bears an illuminating resemblance to the transcendent Deity represented in the Reformed tradition [in the] sense of a powerful Other, of that on which things ultimately depend, to which all are ultimately related, which both limits and sustains human activities.'[152] Wittgenstein, of course, never offers a characterization of

God; moreover, Shields is limiting Wittgenstein to his Tractarian line of thought and he equates logical form with God's will, as if God and logic are external and ultimately hidden strictures to which everything else must fit.

Once the focus is set upon abstractions, the natural question is, 'How do we bridge the gap between these abstractions and our physical world?' If we are going to build a bridge, we need a foundation. Rationalists, such as Descartes, hold that some basic beliefs are a result of rational thought, while empiricists, such as Locke, hold that basic beliefs are a result of gaining knowledge through sense experiences. Yet the influence of Descartes' distinction between consciousness and reality is also found in empiricism where Locke, for example, also thinks that we only have contact with our ideas. There is an external world, but we have access to it only by means of inference from our ideas. Likewise, there is a similarity with Platonic thought in terms of the primacy of ideas in contrast to the fleeting world and our misleading senses. Neither the Cartesian view nor the Platonic view gives full credit to the human condition of living in the world and gaining knowledge in the world.

It is worthwhile to note briefly the arguments of evidentialism and Reformed epistemology, or the so-called Christian philosophy, not because they use Wittgenstein's philosophy, but because they provide examples contrary to his thought. From a Wittgensteinian perspective, they end up with confused arguments since they do not give credit to our religious ways of acting and instead turn to reason and abstractions.

What has been labelled Classical foundationalism holds that some propositions are properly basic and some are not, if not, then the proposition can be rationally accepted only if there is evidence that can be tracked back to what is properly basic. Hence, basic beliefs are the foundation and reason is the mode. Evidentialism is a form of foundationalism that argues that basic beliefs must be either self-evident, such as logical syllogism, or evident to our senses. For example, Locke argues that a rational person will not hold any proposition with greater certainty than the proofs that support it will warrant.[153] It then follows, for Locke, that

the visible marks of extraordinary Wisdom and Power, appear so plainly in all the Works of Creation, that a rational Creature, who will but seriously reflect on them, cannot miss the discovery of a Deity . . . it seems stranger to me, that a whole Nation of Men should be any where found so brutish, as to want the Notion of a God; than that they should be without any Notion of Numbers, or Fire.[154]

God is never directly perceived, only the idea of God, but reason nonetheless discerns that there is a God. Given the evidence, Locke concludes that religious belief is the best explanation of that evidence. His particular form of evidentialism concerning theistic propositions obviously follows his general foundationalist epistemology, that is, he focuses on the ability of reason to discern the nature and reality of God behind the symbols in the world as self-evident.

On the other hand, when Bertrand Russell was asked what he would say if he actually ended up in heaven in front of God, he replied, 'Not enough evidence God! Not enough evidence!'[155] Who is right? Who has the best evidence and results? Locke or Russell? This shows the problem of equating religious beliefs with empirical truth and religious forms of life with the scientific method. In a sense, Russell is the one that sees this accurately, that is, if religious belief is held up as being properly basic in empirical terms, then he is perfectly right to dismiss it. This does not imply that there is no God; it means that evidentialism cannot show that there is a God.

If the evidentialist arguments are rejected, then are there better arguments? Reformed epistemology, like Wittgenstein, rejects classical foundationalism and evidentialism. The Reformed epistemologist, such as Alvin Plantinga, says the possibility of the evidentialist's judgements require a criterion of basicality, but no such criteria has ever been produced, even though the evidentialist says self-evident propositions and incorrigible propositions of sense experience are foundational.[156] The Reformed epistemologist asks how? It is not self-evident that this is so. There is no obvious method or investigation that shows with certainty what is foundational; rather, it is taken for granted. Why can't belief in God be taken for granted? What the Reformed epistemologist is really arguing is that the atheist foundationalist cannot judge religious belief to be false.

The Reformed epistemologist says we cannot have the foundational criteria that the evidentialists seek, but rather than concluding that we cannot believe in God the criteria is changed. The Reformed epistemologist argues that the believer can place belief in God as foundational in and of itself without the requisite evidence since there is no argument for what are basic beliefs in the first place. Despite rightly attacking foundationalism and the idea that religious epistemic practices need to be justified by evidence, they nonetheless insist that belief in God is not groundless, it is basic. Note the distinction between evidentialists – the strength of a religious belief relies on objective evidence and a rational argument – and reformed epistemology – rational belief is not based on evidence, but on basic beliefs.

More specifically, Plantinga uses Calvin to secure his basic beliefs, who notes, 'The knowledge of God has been naturally implanted in the human mind.'[157] Indeed, Wolterstorff says that believing in God entails, as Calvin insists, that we function according to our design.[158] This is certainly true! Given that no general principle could be found to justify religious believe *via* foundationalism and evidentialism, the natural choice is to turn to God. Perhaps as Descartes does as well. Descartes says he is certain that there are 'primary seeds of truth naturally implanted in human minds'.[159] Now the Reformed epistemologists have a general and universal principle to judge the matter. Therefore, if you do not believe in God, it is not because God forgot to implant such an idea in your mind when you were created; rather, sin has covered this innate idea. Since belief in God is said to be part of one's noetic structure, it then follows that evidence is not used or required to prove that belief in God is justified since that very belief is basic.

The Reformed epistemologist bypasses practices and the world and assumes that it is possible to grasp the divine immediately by reason. Consequently, the religious form of life depends on the basic belief of innate knowledge. Wittgenstein, however, shows how religious belief is intimately tied to a form of life and all that surrounds it without either taking the precedent. Hence, meaning is internal rather than external to practices. The theology of glory is an apt candidate for Heschel's criticism: 'philosophers have traditionally adopted the procedure prevalent in general ontology, in which the notion of existence that served as a subject matter of analysis was derived from the realm of inanimate rather than from the realm of animate and personal existence.'[160] As Wittgenstein notes, 'philosophical problems arise when language goes on holiday. And here we may indeed fancy naming to be some remarkable act of mind, as it were a baptism of an object.'[161] According to Wittgenstein, we cannot grasp meaning and language without it working in our lives. To understand religious belief and God we need to look to the religious form of life, the retreat into innate principles or general reason misses what is meant to be understood. If you want to understand music, you must engage instruments, scores and performances. Wittgenstein brings us back from metaphysical flights back to our everyday world.

The post-liberal school of theology rejects the former liberal emphasis on rationalism (and thereby diverges from evidentialism and Reformed epistemology as well) and romanticism and turns to issues in culture and language. Therefore, the post-liberal theologian is moving closer to Wittgenstein; indeed, Wittgenstein's philosophy of language in particular has fuelled the work of George Lindbeck and Hans Frei as they move away from liberal theology. Lindbeck makes good use of Wittgenstein's insights through his study of culture and language, but he uses Wittgenstein more to shed light on aspects of his theory than in a holistic manner. Lindbeck wants to use Wittgenstein's grammatical thoughts in ecumenical discussion since he thinks it allows him to progress towards ecumenical reconciliation without resorting to doctrinal capitulation. In other words, previous theories have failed to promote ecumenical success, whereas his theory might succeed. This intention is, of course, un-Wittgensteinian even without knowing the details. Wittgenstein would never agree that his philosophy should lead to ecumenical success, nor would he agree that it should build another theory.

The problem that Lindbeck sees in former theological theories is that they treat religious beliefs as if they are based on informative propositions which ultimately link with an ontological truth, as if there is a sort of science at work and propositions refer to objective facts, and the truth of the proposition depends on its correspondence to states of affairs. Logical Positivism is known for denying that there can be any such correspondence in terms of religious belief. In light of this criticism, an alternative theory is that religious beliefs are not really saying anything about the real state of affairs; instead, they are inner attitudes and feelings.

Lindbeck rightly sees the problems in these two styles of thought that he labels, cognitive-propositional and experiential-expressive. Both of these hold to a type of foundationalism. The propositionalist (cognitive-propositionalist) generally understands language and practices as directed towards an independent divine reality. Lindbeck notes, 'Religions are thus thought of as similar to philosophy or science as these were classically conceived.'[162] That is, propositions become the focus since they are, if true, reflections of an objective reality. Lindbeck rightly critiques the cognitive approach along Wittgensteinian lines by showing that propositions are not isolated and unmediated.

The pietistic (experiential-expressive) style, on the other hand, does not build a cognitive frame; instead, it focuses on the expressive nature of one's inner life. Lindbeck is right to reject the plausibility of the 'experiential-expressive approach' as he notes, 'because this core experience is said to be common to a wide diversity of religions, it is difficult or impossible to specify its distinctive features, and yet unless this is done, the assertion of commonality becomes logically and empirically vacuous.'[163] This is where Lindbeck makes good use of Wittgenstein's private language argument. The experiential account of pietism, for example, falls on account of religious experience necessarily requiring ritual and worship as the basis for the possibility of religious experience, if you remove the context then what experience are you left with? Of course, just as you cannot separate religious experience from a religious context, so you cannot separate the context from the experience.

The cognitive and experiential theories focus on what is outside the text and practices, that is, they focus on a reality outside the text such as the divine reality or on one's inner experiences. In both cases, the outer divine reality and inner experience are *a priori* while the text and practices follow. Instead, religion, like language, is understood through a cultural context that is the medium preceding inner experiences and fosters the language that then forms our religious understanding. You cannot remove religious practice as secondary to meaning. For Lindbeck, just as language exists before the individual, rituals and religion exist before the individual, and in both cases it is never experiences that are the basis of meaning. Therefore, doctrines on God are not first-order truth statements; they are second-order statements that set the context and rules for how to speak about God. Lindbeck carries a sound argument against pietism that is generally in accord with Wittgenstein's thought.

Given Lindbeck's desire for ecumenical success, he argues that it cannot be reached by means of the propositionalist or pietistic theories. The propositionalist theory cannot achieve it since their cognitive focus on doctrines is immutable; and the pietistic theory has little regard for doctrine. He tries to avoid the problems of doctrine being understood as a means to define truths that correspond to a divine reality, and he tries to avoid doctrine being understood as a manifestation of an inner experience. According to Lindbeck, what is lacking in ecumenical dialogue is the right theory, so his move is to argue for the right theory, as he claims: 'there would be less scepticism about ecumenical claims if it were possible to find an alternative approach that made the intertwining of variability and invariability in matters of faith easier to understand. This book proposes such an alternative.'[164] Lindbeck proposes the 'cultural-linguistic' and 'intratextualism' approaches as an alternate theory and general way of conceptualizing religion.[165]

Lindbeck says: 'Intratexual theology redescribes reality within the scriptural framework rather than translating Scripture into extrascriptural categories. It is the text, so to speak, which absorbs the world, rather than the world the text.'[166] This approach is thought, by Lindbeck, to help ecumenical dialogue since it negates the idea that we need to be concerned with a correspondence to reality, whereby doctrines are not simply truth claims or expressive manifestations in symbols; rather, they are community authoritative doctrines. He places this as analogical to the way 'genetic codes or computer programs may remain identical even while producing startling different products depending on input and situation, so also with the basic grammars of cultures, languages, and religions.'[167] In this way, he hopes that the ecumenical community will see that their doctrine need not be understood in terms of a submit or reject dichotomy. Rather, there is a flux in understanding differences, as he notes between driving on the left or right, neither is to be changed, just understood when applied in differing circumstances – hence the doctrine is not really altered.[168]

Lindbeck is right to point out that an independent reality in religion is not some isolated factor and that we must look to the forms of life, yet he turns to what he calls the 'Ultimately Real'. As if the 'Ultimately Real' makes it clear that he is referring to something outside the variable doctrines, while a discussion of God or Jesus may not! This seems to imply that there is still correspondence in his theory, even though he apparently wanted to rid his theory of correspondence. Is the 'genetic code' he mentions the 'Ultimately Real'? There could be a remaining correspondence in his theory between the genetic code and the resultant religion, and remember we probably cannot know the genetic code in the case of religion.

Lindbeck seems to think that his term 'intrasystematic truth' replaces the problematic ontological truth, yet he still maintains a correspondence to the 'Most Important' and the 'Ultimately Real'. He says, 'the great strength of a cognitive-propositional theory of religion is that . . . it admits the possibility of such truth claims, and a crucial theological challenge to a cultural-linguistic approach is whether it also can do so.'[169] Lindbeck seems to think that a statement, such as 'Christ is Lord', corresponds to reality with some objective truth and without mediation through practices. Oddly, he notes: 'There is nothing in the cultural-linguistic approach that requires the rejection (or acceptance) of the epistemological realism and correspondence theory of truth, which, according to most of the theological tradition, is implicit in the conviction of believers that when they rightly use a sentence such as "Christ is Lord" they are uttering a true first-order proposition.'[170] Lindbeck posits the diversity of community formed doctrines, but behind them all is the one doctrine of a realist fashion. This is similar to the case of linguistic idealism, where language is said to be formed by people, but ultimately it falls back to realism since we might place a Platonic language behind all. Although Lindbeck tries to evade the propositional model of religious language, he nonetheless maintains it with his reference to the 'Ultimate' – which seems similar to the hidden God.

Lindbeck is in the odd situation of promoting the community and practices, yet devaluing them in light of his 'genetic code' and the 'ultimately real'. He seems to think that there is one doctrine, but it is expressed in differing ways. Doctrines are not, as Lindbeck seems to think, differing unmediated descriptions of the 'Ultimately Real'. If ecumenical progress rests on the assumption of this 'Ultimately Real', then what is it? If it is only a theory, then what is the nature of the ecumenical unity? Is it simply a common agreement that despite the differences we are the same underneath? This is like the story of several blind people being directed to an elephant to feel it and describe it, and the response is that an elephant is a tree, a wall, a rope, etc., depending on the part they grasped. To hold this latter notion is analogous to a type of modalism, where the one doctrine beyond takes various forms in various communities, none of which is accurate or the truth in any clear sense. Just as modalism in theology does not give any credit to the distinction of three persons in the Trinity, in this example, no credit is given to different doctrines and practices.

A doctrinal disagreement is really a disagreement in worship, not some underlying unity. Although Lindbeck wants to work from the specific contexts of religion, he nonetheless ties that context to the 'Ultimately Real'. This tie to the separated 'Ultimately Real' is not mediated in any fashion; he has taken flight from the language-games and practices. Theology cannot be so easily weaned into ecumenical agreement since doing so will also affect the communities' practices. Lindbeck wants to provide the way to solve doctrinal disputes without doctrinal capitulation, but that would entail, from a Wittgensteinian view, a unity of practices since they are intimately tied to doctrine. It is interesting to note that while the Reformed epistemologists view practices as expressions of a reality that lies beyond practices, those like Lindbeck, view social expressions of a religion as representing a doctrinal unity beyond them. In both cases, there is a foundation outside our everyday lives.

Lindbeck rightly denies the validity of the cognitive-propositional and experiential-expressive theories, and he takes a Wittgensteinian turn towards community, but he seems to end up denying the mediation of the communities' language and practices since what he regards as important is the underlying 'Ultimate Real' that is reflected in various ways. Lindbeck uses Wittgenstein to support his cultural-linguistic theory, but it assumes that there is one foundational unity underlying all the different expressions of that unity, and he consequently posits a theory that maintains vestiges of realism – all of which is un-Wittgensteinian. It is a mistake to regard religious practices as secondarily tied to a doctrinal foundation that is unmediated and external to our life. This devaluing of practices allows Lindbeck and others to think that if we see past the differences in practice then we can see the unity that is behind and external to them. Lindbeck seeks ecumenical unity, an underlying unity, that will help ease disputes, but Wittgenstein wants to show the nature of disputes, he wants to show differences. He notes, 'Hegel seems to me to be always wanting to say that things which look different are really the same. Whereas my interest is in showing that things which look the same are really different.'[171]

The Evangelical Kevin Vanhoozer critiques Lindbeck, and the Post-liberal Yale School connection generally, for using Wittgenstein to locate meaning in the community rather than some other reference.[172] Vanhoozer says:

> Strictly speaking, it is not the story as such but the way in which it is used that is doctrinally normative. Where does this pattern of use come from? Unfortunately, Lindbeck does not say. Lindbeck concurs with Frei's construal of the Bible's literal sense in terms of the consensus tradition of Scripture's use rather than in terms of its 'nature' as realistic narrative.[173]

The problem seen by Vanhoozer is that ontology and realism are coming into question in favour of community and practices. Vanhoozer says, 'Lindbeck draws a crucial distinction between a story and its use, a distinction that derives from a mistaken application of Wittgenstein's dictum that "meaning is use" and

"Practice gives the words their sense".' Additionally, 'Lindbeck takes a fateful step beyond Wittgenstein's account, however, when he suggests that the meaning of stories is similarly a function of their community use. To equate the meaning of a narrative with its use is to collapse the story's intratextual meaning into its reception in an interpretive community.'[174] Vanhoozer thereby considers Lindbeck as devaluing doctrine and putting the cart before the horse, that is, he puts the community before doctrine. Consequently, 'Lindbeck's so-called postliberal approach here finds itself with a surprising bedfellow: the archliberal Friedrich Schleiermacher. Whereas for Schleiermacher doctrines are religious affects put forth in speech, doctrines for Lindbeck are articulations of meaning and logic of habitual Christian practices.'[175]

In contrast to the community centred belief, Vanhoozer directs us to a canonical centred belief. He says, 'The present study aims to correct . . . this cultural-linguistic misstep by locating authority not in the use of scripture by the believing community but in what Nicholas Wolterstorff calls divine authorial discourse.'[176] It is clear that Vanhoozer wants to set up revelation as taking the precedent, and then practices follow, while he thinks Lindbeck demotes the precedent of scripture and ultimately supports an ecclesial expressivism. Vanhoozer thinks he avoids this problem through his canonical-linguistic theology since it sees the priority of the canon over 'its relationship to reality' and the 'canonical before communal'.[177] For Vanhoozer, it is 'the text which absorbs the world, rather than the world the text'.[178] Vanhoozer, like Reformed epistemology, places a priority on an external ontological reality.

Vanhoozer's emphasis on the text is extraordinary; does he think that the text pre-dates religion? Was there any religion prior to the text? The text is not exactly a heavenly entity that then appeared at the beginning of time and human history. The text is more roughshod than Vanhoozer imagines. Does God really make grammatical mistakes? Did God change his first language from Hebrew to Greek? Perhaps Vanhoozer's understanding of the text is more similar to some schools of Judaism and Islam, where there have been debates regarding the possibility of an eternal heavenly text. However, not only is the text given some ideal setting, so is reason. The notion of trying to understand the text requires a divine ability if we do not understand it through the community. Thus, Vanhoozer follows Plantinga and Calvin by postulating that there is an innate reason and understanding that we all have, but has been hampered by sin since the Fall of humankind.[179]

The difference between Vanhoozer and Lindbeck is similar to that between the Alexandrians and Antiochians – they see the other through their own apologetic lens. The Alexandrians accuse the Antiochians of emphasizing the human nature too greatly, and the Antiochians accuse the Alexandrians of emphasizing the divine nature too greatly. Likewise, Lindbeck can be likened to either a Eutychian or Ebionite Christology. I suggest that Lindbeck is more Eutychian because he transmutes the different religious practices and communities into an abstract 'Ultimate Reality'. However, since Vanhoozer tends towards realism, I think he would take the opposite view and classify Lindbeck as Ebionite because, from his point of view, Lindbeck reduces an ontological truth found in the text to the human community. Likewise, the Ebionites reduce Christ to a human who is not attached in any substantial manner to an ontological divine nature. In short: Lindbeck is an advocate of cultural-linguistic theology and Vanhoozer is an advocate of canonical-linguistic theology. Thus, the battle of theories and labels wages on.

The theology of the cross

The theology of glory searches for an Archimedean point to secure a theory, be it properly basic beliefs, the 'Ultimately Real', or a canonical-linguistic text. In contrast, earthly life and practices are thought to be secondary and only symbols that hopefully refer to an external reality and God, and none of which are in full communication – including the incarnation. These foundational type points move our attention away from seeing the central role that practices play. This thought is not, however, unique to theology; it is also found in secular investigations. For example, Russell's analytical search ends with sense data to free his investigation from subjectivity and to secure meaning. In a similar fashion, Wittgenstein's early work links meaning to simple objects and Plato's Good was the basis of the plurality of Forms. Interestingly, Nietzsche notes, 'Where man cannot find anything to see or grasp, he has no further business – that is certainly an imperative different from the Platonic one . . . we have nothing but rough work to do.'[180] And as Wittgenstein notes, 'We have got on to slippery ice where there is no friction and so in a certain sense the conditions are ideal, but also, just because of that, we are unable to walk. We want to walk: so we need friction. Back to the rough ground!'[181]

Wittgenstein's later work rejects the type of thought found in the theology of glory and instead is more closely associated with theologians such as Irenaeus, Tertullian and Luther. Luther describes the theology of the cross: 'That person does not deserve to be called a theologian who looks upon the invisible things of God as though they were clearly perceptible'; rather, 'he deserves to be called a theologian, however, who comprehends the visible and manifest things of God seen through suffering and the cross.'[182] Luther does not deny that God's power, wisdom, majesty, etc., may be surmised from creation. What he does deny is that such knowledge has any use. In philosophy and theology, the invisible and abstract is exactly that, it is not of use. It makes us 'neither worthy nor wise'. While the theology of glory focuses on the invisible God behind creation and attaches labels such as powerful, wise, etc. (perhaps a giant in the sky), the theology of the cross turns towards the visible God in human weakness and suffering. In effect, to delve into abstractions is nobody's view, it is the invisible inferred God.

Likewise, Tertullian writes:

What is there in common between Athens and Jerusalem? Between the Academy and the church? Our system of beliefs (*institution*) comes from the Porch of Solomon, who himself taught that it was necessary to seek God in the simplicity of the heart. So much worse for those who talk of a 'stoic', 'platonic', or 'dialectic' Christianity! We have no need for curiosity after Jesus Christ, nor for inquiry (inquisition) after the gospel. When we believe, we desire to believe nothing further. For we believe nothing more than 'there is nothing else which we are obliged to believe'.[183]

Like Luther, Tertullian, sees that a Greek style search for God goes beyond the given, but it does so because this view devalues the given. Wittgenstein notes, the visible world seems to be too insignificant compared to invisible things:

> It is very *remarkable* that we should be inclined to think of civilization – houses, trees, cars, etc. – as separating man from his origins, from what is lofty and eternal, etc. Our civilized environment, along with it trees and plants, strikes us then as though it were cheaply wrapped in cellophane and isolated from everything great, from God, as it were. That is a remarkable picture that intrudes on us.[184]

Wittgenstein once noted that his method could be summed up as the opposite of that of Socrates, that is, in the Platonic dialogues Socrates seeks to answer questions such as 'What is knowledge?' by searching for something that all examples of knowledge have in common. Wittgenstein consequently notes:

> It has puzzled me why Socrates is regarded as a great philosopher. Because when Socrates asks for the meaning of a word and people give him examples of how that word is used, he isn't satisfied but wants a unique definition. Now if someone shows me how a word is used and its different meanings that is just the sort of answer I want.[185]

Likewise, as Rhees says, 'When Plato speaks of the form of the good in the *Republic*, he does not say that the sensible world, and earthly life, is any sort of imitation or likeness of that. He insists that there cannot be any representation or appearance of the good.'[186] As long as we keep language idling with, for example, abstract notions of 'Good' it is impossible to understand the term

'Good', and as long as we keep God isolated as an abstraction, it is impossible to understand God.

Lindbeck may fall into this Socratic confusion when he notes, 'What we assert, in other words, is that "God is good" is meaningful and true but without knowing the meaning of "God is good".'[187] The problem is that he is referring to some sort of metaphysics of good, in which case it is impossible to grasp what the word means since it has no application. On the other hand, Wittgenstein says, 'Could you explain the concept of the punishments of hell without using the concept of punishment? Or that of God's goodness without using the concept of goodness? If you want to get the right effect with your words, certainly not.'[188] Remember, as previously noted, the language-games are interconnected, they are not completely independent, thus, we know what being good is in our daily lives. Just as Wittgenstein wants 'to bring words back from their metaphysical to their everyday application'[189] the theology of the cross wants to bring the Word back from the metaphysical to the physical application. In other words, the language-games mediate our contact with reality as Christ mediates our contact with God.

Once again, Wittgenstein says, 'if the place I want to get to could only be reached by way of a ladder, I would give up trying to get there. For the place I really have to get to is a place I must already be right now. Anything that I might reach by climbing a ladder does not interest me.'[190] Phillip tries to climb this ladder when he says to Jesus, 'Show us the Father.' Jesus' reply rejects this looking elsewhere and turns Phillip back to him, 'He who has seen me has seen the Father' (John 14.8). What is important is what God has actually done in this world, not what he could or might do in abstraction. Dietrich Bonhoeffer insightfully observes that we understand the 'Divine, not in absolutes, but in the natural form of man'.[191] We are not in a position to build ladders to God or to metaphysical foundations and then debate the best explanatory ladder. Rather, the hidden God (*Deus absconditus*) becomes the revealed God (*Deus revelatus*) in Jesus Christ and throws the ladder out at the same time.

In contrast to beginning from above with Greek thought and divine attributes, we need to start on the rough ground. Luther says, 'The scriptures begin very gently, and lead us on to Christ as to a man, and then to the one who is Lord over all creatures, and after that to one who is God. So do I enter delightfully and learn to know God. But the philosophers and doctors have insisted on beginning from above.'[192] As Luther says, 'the real knowledge of God, unlike metaphysical speculation, one must gain in a "practical" manner.'[193] Likewise, Wittgenstein comes to realize that logic is understood practically, 'You must look at the practice of language then you will see it.'[194] Practice is essential to Wittgenstein's philosophy, and to theology; neither is properly a matter of epistemology or apologetics. Jesus says in Matthew, for example, 'Go and tell John what you hear and see' in accord with the Isaiah theme of needing the ears and eyes of faith.

Consequently, theologians do not properly deal with epistemological questions such as the existence of God in abstraction. Even the so-called proofs of God's existence are set after believing that there is a God. Instead, the nature of theology is to note grammatical distinctions and practices, what we do, see and hear. Wittgenstein notes:

> Luther said that theology is the grammar of the word
> 'God'. I interpret this to mean that an investigation of
> the word would be a grammatical one. For example,
> people might dispute about how many arms God had,
> and someone might enter the dispute by denying that one
> could talk about arms of God. This would throw light on
> the use of the word. What is ridiculous or blasphemous
> also shows the grammar of the word.[195]

What we do and do not say about God is not determined in abstraction, as Luther notes, grammar is fixed to our lives and practices:

> tell me what language has there ever been that men have
> successfully learned to speak as a result of grammatical
> rules? Are not rather those languages that adhere most
> closely to rules, such as Greek and Latin, nevertheless
> learned by using them? Therefore how great a folly it is
> in the instance of sacred language, where theological and

spiritual matters are treated, to disregard the particular character of the subject matter to arrive at the sense on the basis of grammatical rules![196]

Look to the practice, then you will see meaning, logic and God in their respective ways.

Chapter 7

Wittgenstein in Theological Practice

Climbing the ladder of reason beyond practices is effectively blinding, not because of the great realization at the top, but because there is nothing to see. Wittgenstein's philosophy and Chalcedonian Christology provide a useful basis to discuss the central role of history and practices on the 'rough ground' through the examples of Scripture, the sacrament of the Lord's Supper and the Church. The following Nestorian and Eutychian points of view represent tendencies within theological discourse rather than any one particular perspective. This section should show that there is no need to develop further theories supplemented by Wittgenstein's philosophy to address theology; rather, his philosophy can stand on its own and speak to core subjects in theology. These initial considerations that follow are intended to foster further discussions on Wittgenstein and theology.

Scripture

In the previous chapters, the philosophical question that arose concerned the relationship between ideas and the external world, and the theological question concerned the relationship between the human and divine attributes. The biblical text naturally draws on these relationships since it is traditionally regarded as a human text in terms of its context (i.e. it fits into human history and has human writers) while at the same time it is God's Word. Consequently, we can ask in Christological fashion, how do these two attributes relate to each other? Is the text providing concrete truths concerning our empirical world? Is the text providing symbolic representations of a divine reality beyond it? It is well known that Antioch (Nestorius) is associated with literal interpretation and that Alexandria (Eutyches) is associated with allegorical interpretation. Although there is not a strict division between these two forms of interpretation in practice, I will keep them distinct in order to show the differences between them more clearly.

A Nestorian view maintains the separation between the human and divine and regards the text as the means through which God provides distinct rules and knowledge about our physical world. Just as Christ is a real human, the text speaks about our real world. Since it is God who addresses our world through the text it must necessarily follow that the text provides truths about our world. This viewpoint can lead to the notion that the text provides legalist rules and even scientific evidence. For example, 'How old is the earth?' 'Was the world created in six days?' The Nestorian and Biblicist view could conclude that six days is a truth statement and then proceed – in light of the direct correlation between the truth statements of the text and our world – to explain how geology in fact proves this correlation. Would this depiction of the text do it justice? Would a congregation, upon hearing that there are natural explanations for God's work and that the Bible is, in a sense, a science text, find that it deepens their faith?

The union between the divine and human natures in Nestorian Christology is one of pragmatics and morals, not substantiality. Likewise, the union between the physical text and God is one of pragmatics and morals. The text provides dogmatic, historical and scientific truths along with moral imperatives. In both cases, what can become the focus is the rationality of these truths and functions. What may be lost, to some extent, is a substantial relationship – beginning with the Nestorian Christology and now with the text. Perhaps the Nestorian view of the incarnation and the text, in light of the strict separation, is representative of a divorce – whereby the relationship is, at best, a matter of functional legalities. Indeed, it is possible that the emphasis on the pragmatic nature of the text can take precedence over Christ. Of course, few, if anyone, would admit to this. However, the text as a source book of truths also includes statements about Christ, and by proving that it is error free (including facts such as the age of the earth), it then adds reasonability to the belief in Christ. Thus, the text plays a foundational role similar role to Descartes' *cogito ergo sum*, from which a Nestorian oriented theology can build further knowledge.

Alternatively, a Eutychian view may see the text as a representative reflection of the divine. The words of the text are symbols that refer to divine truths. Christ must be purely divine and the text must be purely true, but this state cannot be found in our world; therefore, the text and Christ must be transmuted beyond our world. It is on this point that textual history loses significance as unchanging transcendent truths gain significance. This is the point of the allegorical method, to transmute the straightforward text into transcendent truths. You must go beyond the human and physical to higher truth, like the Platonic striving to rise above words as mere reflections of transcendent Forms. Consequently, a Eutychian oriented theology sees the role of the interpreter (i.e. theologian) as discovering the intellectual truths outside the text. The text stripped of its context becomes a mirror of the interpreter's metaphysical musings.

In contrast to the Nestorian and Eutychian viewpoints, the Chalcedonian perspective sees the text as God's Word written by human authors along with their human limits and attributes. Thus, the text is not super-human knowledge about the empirical world, and it is not symbolic knowledge beyond the human world. Instead, the text joins meaning in the material and spiritual together. The text thereby carries the Christological aspect of being distinctly God's Word with a distinctly human context in full communication. Is this rational? No. Is the incarnation rational? No. However, it is not the philosopher's transcendent truths or the scientist's empirical truths that the text provides; it is Christ, 'I am Truth!' Wittgenstein remarks, 'If you can accept the miracle that God became man, then all these [textual] difficulties are as nothing. For then it is impossible for me to say what form the record of such an event should take.'[197] There is a similarity between God taking on the form of a servant and the cross, and using human speech along with its errors.

In contrast to the Eutychian view, the physical and worldly narrative of salvation history is the given, not transcendent truths. The text is not a book that directs us out of the cave of shadows to eternal and immutable truths; rather, it is in history and the physical world that God works the salvation of human-kind. In contrast to the Nestorian view, the text is not a history or science textbook. Perhaps the written word obscures the fact that these are living words in a living community, they are not simply archaic written documents or a textbook of proofs and explanations. Wittgenstein rightly observes, '*Here you have a narrative, don't take the same attitude to it as you take to other historical narratives!* Make a *quite different* place in your life for it.'[198] Viewing the text as the source of empirical truths and moral lessons misses the living aspect of the Word. As Luther empha-sizes, 'that's why the evangelists wrote the history poorly and gave little attention to the words, in order that they might tear us away from the history and lead us to the benefit.' 'We want, however, to set it into an order of events.' However, 'Paul, Peter and the other apostles did not bother themselves much with the order and history of the Resurrection, but empha-sized much greater their power and benefit.'[199] Wittgenstein likewise says,

> the historical accounts of the Gospels might, historically
> speaking, be demonstrably false and yet belief would
> lose nothing by this: *not*, however, because it concerns
> 'universal truths of reason'! Rather, because historical
> proof (the historical proof-game) is irrelevant to
> belief. This message (the Gospels) is seized on by
> men believingly (i.e. lovingly). *That* is the certainty
> characterizing this particular acceptance–as–true, not
> something *else*.[200]

This must be understood correctly, Wittgenstein does not say this history is false. What he says, is that the exact details of history do not help us in any manner, yet at the same time the history is important in contrast to transcendent truths. The importance of history rejects the Eutychian view, and the importance of the culmination of history rejects the Nestorian view. The text is not approached as strictly literalist (Nestorian) or allegorical (Eutychian) since history and its culmination are distinct yet remain intimately joined.

Sacrament: the Lord's Supper

During the Reformation a debate, largely between Zwingli and Luther, centred on the word 'is' since Jesus says, 'this is my body' and 'this is my blood' at the Last Supper. Does 'is' literally mean 'is', or does it mean 'signifies'? In the first instance, the debate may have the appearance of a linguistic disagreement; however, it is better understood as a Christological disagreement. For example, the Nestorian analogy argues that the bread and wine of the Supper are symbols of a divine reality – the word 'is' signifies. The Eutychian analogy argues that the bread and wine are Christ's body and blood – the word 'is' is literal. In the former, Christ is at best spiritually present; in the latter, he is also physically present.

The Nestorian analogy generally fits the Reformed tradition. As was shown previously in terms of Nestorian Christology, this tradition does not allow the full communication of attributes between the divine and human natures of Christ. Indeed, from the Reform perspective the full communication of attributes is illogical. How can Christ, who is in heaven at the right hand of the Father, be physically present at even one Lord's Supper celebration, let alone torn asunder to all the celebrations? Impossible! Consequently, the external elements of bread and wine are symbols that signify a spiritual reality to which faith is directed. As Zwingli says, 'for the gaining of salvation I attribute no power to any elements of this world, that is, things of sense . . . For body and spirit are such essentially different things that whichever one you take it cannot be the other.'[201] The platonic notion that the transcendent cannot have a full and complete expression in the world is similar to the reformed axiom that the finite is not capable of the infinite. Neither Christ nor the Lord's Supper can hold a substantial union of the divine and human natures.

The Eutychian analogy carries the notion of what has been named transubstantiation and is typically associated with the Catholic tradition. This position argues that the bread and wine are no longer present since they are transmuted into Christ's body and blood. All that remains of the bread and wine is the look, taste and feel of bread and wine. This position has been

characterized as drawing too strongly on the Aristotelian principles of essence and accident to explain how the elements can
have the accidents of looking like bread and wine but are essentially Christ's body and blood. Likewise, Eutychian Christology
argues that Christ has only the accidents of appearing to be
human, but essentially he is divine. It is clearly extraordinary
to regard bread as the body of Christ and wine as the blood of
Christ; likewise, it is extraordinary to regard Jesus as God. Both
the Nestorian and Eutychian views see this, but they resolve it in
inverse directions (just as Locke and Berkeley did in philosophy
concerning the separation of ideas and substance). Consequently,
they both deny a substantial union, the former through strict
separation and the latter though transmutation.

A Chalcedonian view of the Lord's Supper would keep the
distinct nature of the physical elements (against the Eutychian
view) and at the same time keep the distinct nature of the divine
in a substantial union (against the Nestorian view). However, the
Nestorian perspective would not only regard this to be impossible, it would also be undignified. Indeed, it would be close to
idolatry since the divine is attached to something that it cannot
be. However, Luther says,

> The glory of our God is precisely that for our sakes he
> comes down to the very depths, into human flesh, into
> bread, into our mouths, our heart, our bosom: moreover,
> for our sakes he allows himself to be treated ingloriously
> both on the cross and on the altar, as St. Paul says in
> 1 Corinthians 11 that some eat the bread in an unworthy
> manner.[202]

The 'inglorious' aspect that Luther mentions does not simply
reside in Christ becoming bread, or for that matter becoming
human, it resides in the role of Christ as the suffering servant.
The Lord's Supper removes the ladder and shows the true meaning of spiritual, that is, not something removed from us that we
know not what, or that to which we must ascend; rather, it is
here in the material world. As was shown in the theology of the
cross, it is not the transcendence and glory but the suffering and
rough ground that show God.

Often we view the world as inferior to the divine, just as the bread and wine are inferior to Christ, but if we see that creation itself includes the divine presence – instead of supporting a dualistic position – then it should be clearer that the divine can be in the material. Likewise, Wittgenstein rejects the idea that logic is an *a priori* and ideal foundation outside our use of language; it and language are in an internal relationship. This does not mean, of course, that the whole world is one sacrament, or that there is one language; it means that there is one place that the Word is uniquely addressing us, and that there are unique language-games. However, the Nestorian view, despite agreeing that God is present everywhere, does not admit to the full communication of attributes; therefore, it is impossible for Christ to be present everywhere (except as divided in a spiritual sense) so the elements signify Christ. That is, they are a sign of Christ. Consequently, the Lord's Supper is based on the remembrance of Christ and, at best, the presence of the spiritual Christ. The word 'is' directs us away from the elements and a physical presence towards the mental and spiritual.

Wittgenstein rejects ostensive definition and shows that understanding words requires seeing them in practice. This applies to the Lord's Supper. The phrase 'this is my body' is not an ostensive definition since understanding it necessarily requires understanding the activity associated with it. If this phrase was merely an ostensive definition, and it only meant that the bread I am pointing to is Christ's body and the wine is Christ's blood, then we might ask. What is he doing there while physically present? Is he relaxing on the altar? However, the meaning here is not mere physical presence and pointing, it is Christ in action – redemptive action. Therefore, the basis of Lord's Supper does not simply amount to pointing to the bread and saying it is Christ's body and then adoring it; rather, the basis is the redemptive action of his body and blood at the cross. Consequently, the Lord's Supper is not located in our act and practice of remembering and pointing, with our mind or finger, it is Christ's act and practice of forgiveness through his body and blood – it is the spiritual in the material together. Indeed, that is why the Chalcedonian perspective leads to the consequence that even the most ardent rejecter of the sacrament truly eats and drinks Christ's body and blood (albeit possibly not to their bene-fit). The Chalcedonian view directs the individual away from representations and ostensive definitions towards the physical and spiritual activity of Christ.

Church

It is natural to raise Christological questions when discussing the church since it is traditionally understood as the body of Christ. Paul says, 'the church, which is his body' (Ephesians 1.22). Moreover, Saul (later named Paul) persecutes Christians and consequently hears, 'Saul, why do you persecute me?' (Acts 9.4). In other words, persecuting Christians is persecuting Christ because they are his body. Once again, we have the perplex-ing relationship of the divine and physical natures. What is the nature of the church?

A Nestorian perspective of the church leans towards a spir-itualizing tendency. In order to safeguard the church it keeps the divine and physical natures distinct. Consequently, it seems to endorse two churches – the invisible-spiritual church and the visible-physical church. The comparison with Nestorianism's two Christs is obvious. There are two natures, but there is not one substantial union; therefore, there are two distinct iden-tities. Nonetheless, there must be some type of union. The Christological result carries into the church. Since the union is not substantial, it is functional. The visible church is the func-tional arm of the invisible church. The church on earth thereby symbolizes the one in heaven, perhaps including a divinely man-dated organizational structure, and the more it approximates the invisible church the better the copy.

A Eutychian view of the church, in contrast, would under-stand the one visible church as transmuted into the invisible church. This obviously does not mean that the visible becomes invisible; it means that the visible is equated with the spiritual. Consequently, there is one church and the empirical walls of the church are the walls of the heavenly church. Therefore, if you are outside *our* walls, then your salvation is in jeopardy. This view can carry functional components, but a unique difficulty resides in the determination of who really is and is not within these particular walls.

A Chalcedonian view of the church would affirm two distinct natures (in contrast to the Eutychian view) in one church (in contrast to the Nestorian view). In other words, it is a given that the physical church and its members on earth through history are not identical with the church at the culmination of salvation history, yet it is in a substantial union with the divine. The core of the substantial union is based on the Chalcedonian view that the Lord's Supper is Christ's body and blood, and Christ's body is the church. Therefore, the one church is both visible and invisible. It is visible where the Lord's Supper is, yet it is invisible in the sense that the particular members and walls do not circumscribe it. However, the use of the term 'invisible' in this case is misleading since it makes one think of something too spiritual and ethereal, and is best associated with the Nestorian position. A better term is 'hidden' since it more clearly describes the church as not fully visible in its entirety, but that it can nonetheless be seen in the right place and way; namely, the Lord's Supper. In other words, the physical church is not a copy of something external to it; it is both physical and spiritual, it is the body of Christ. Hidden does not imply invisibility, it implies that something visible is not seen because you are not looking in the right place.

This is comparable to the distinction between Wittgenstein's early and later conception of logic. His early understanding of logic, as found in the *Tractatus*, points to an invisible underlying logical syntax (once again, who can see the simple object). Additionally, the Nestorian church is visible to the extent that it mirrors the invisible church that determines it; likewise, Wittgenstein's Tractarian conception of language is that it is understood to the extent that it mirrors the underlying logical structure that determines it. In contrast, Wittgenstein's later understanding of logic is comparable to the Chalcedonian hidden and seen comparison. Language and logic are in a reciprocal relationship; therefore, language is not a visible representation of something external and invisible to it. Consequently, the reason you may not see logic or the church is not because they are an invisible and external foundation, which language and the empirical church copy respectively; rather, it is because you are not looking in the right place in the right way; namely, practices. Recall that Wittgenstein says, 'You must look at the practice of language, then you will see it [logic].'[203]

Doctrines, practices and ecumenical discussions

Rhees notes, 'You cannot have the idea of God apart from religious worship. You could not explain to anyone what we mean by "God" without pointing to all that belongs to religious worship.'[204] This is in accord with the theology of the cross with an emphasis on God shown through practice. In contrast, the theology of glory, due to the separation between the material and spiritual, hides God in abstractions. For example, note that Calvin supports Plato, 'for the very thing which Plato meant when he taught, as he often does, that the chief good of the soul consists in resemblance to God'.[205] Whereas Rhees rightly says,

> in Christianity one's relation to God *is* the worship of God. . . . if anyone should ask what the relation of the creature to God is, then one might most readily point to the worship of God, as if to say: 'Look there, you'll see.' And this is not the sort of thing that is suggested by Plato's idea of becoming as like to the divine as possible. Indeed, it could be said it is just the opposite. When Plato speaks of the form of the good . . . he does not say that the sensible world, and earthly life, is any sort of imitation or likeness of that.[206]

Wittgenstein shows that practice is where meaning is shown, so in theological terms it is not transcendence alone that is significant, it is the practices associated with Christ, the Lord's Supper, etc., that bind the relationship. In other words, it is not only a spiritual relationship; it is also a material relationship. Luther similarly points to the importance of worship practices:

> he who wants to find Christ, must first find the church. How would one know Christ and faith in him if one did

not know where they are who believe in him? He who
would know something concerning Christ, must neither
trust in himself nor build his bridge into heaven by means
of his own reason, but he should go to the church. . . .
The church is not wood and stone but the assembly of
people who believe in Christ. With this church one
should be connected and see how the people believe, live,
and teach.[207]

Religious practice is the context in which belief has its sense;
therefore, if theological meaning is lost it means that the practices are lost, not the definition or transcendent referent.

A discussion that emphasizes concrete practices, in contrast
to ontological truths and abstractions, may be charged with
reductionism since religious belief seems to be reduced to mere
attitudes and associated practices with no external reference.
However, Rhees notes, 'it would be ridiculous to suggest that
religious language was concerned with calling forth certain attitudes. Religious language is concerned with God, with thanking
God, praying to God and praising God. It will not do at all to say
that it is directed toward attitudes.'[208] For example, in the practice
of the Lord's Supper the point is not to partake of the practice of
the Lord's Supper, or of a particular attitude, but of God. God is
not reduced or limited to the practice; God is shown in the practice. Likewise, for Wittgenstein, logic is not based on external
metaphysical structures or an inner idealism. Logic is not reduced
to language practices; rather, logic is shown in language practices. Fergus Kerr rightly observes that the turn away from excessive rationalization does not fall into subjectivism and pietism:
'Wittgenstein's later work strives to show that neither feeling nor
reason but action is the foundational thing. It is consistent with
this that he should lay emphasis on ceremony, on symbolism, in
religion, because it is not "thought up", or to be regarded (nor-
mally) as glimpses of interior spiritual states.'[209] It is just as wrong
to think that God is merely in our attitudes (pietism) as it is to
imagine that the physical world is in our ideas (idealism).

If the focus is removed from ontological truths to practices
then, as noted by Rhees, 'Someone might ask "Well why have

all this theology at all, then? Is it not just so much trellis-work or ornamentation that could as well be left out? Well, consider "To know God is to worship him". What is worshipping God, precisely? Could you speak of worshipping God – would that mean anything – without some sort of theology?'[210] Not only are practices necessary, so is theology. Without mathematics the symbols =, −, ×, etc., have little meaning. The practice of worship and the practice of mathematics are only meaningful with an associated theology and mathematics. Rhees says,

> I say that without this theology religious devotion, reverence and religious exaltation would have no sense at all. And yet – once more – I do not mean that this theology, the learning of these ways of speaking, is what has produced religion. If children learn to speak of God through having the Bible read to them, the Bible itself was the outcome of religion before it was the source of it. In general, one might say that theology grows out of religious devotion just as much as the other way about. And no theology is conceivable except in connection with a religious tradition.[211]

Theology and practice go hand in hand; they are in a reciprocal relationship. Likewise, Wittgenstein's logic and language, and Chalcedonian Christological human and divine natures, are not reduced to one side or the other; instead, there is a union that keeps the distinctions and the substantial nature. Perhaps we could say in logical terms, that the Word has a certain pre-eminence, but we could not have any understanding of the Word in abstraction, only in human and concrete practices. For example, in the case of the Lord's Supper, the Word makes the sacrament, and in terms of logic has a sense of priority, but to elevate the Word beyond the bread contradicts the fact that the Word commands the sacrament, which is the body and blood of the Word. From a Chalcedonian perspective, the Word is not elevated at the expense of the elements, the spiritual is not elevated at the expense of the material, and theology is not elevated at the expense of practices.

Peter Winch rightly says:

> Theological doctrines are not developed independently of their possibilities of application in the worship and religious lives of believers; and these latter have a certain, though not complete, autonomy. I mean that if a doctrine were felt by believers to be hostile to their practices of prayer and worship, that would create a difficulty for the theological doctrine itself. I emphasise that the traffic goes in both directions and there is a give and take. Believers' attitudes towards worship may be modified under pressure of priests, for example, who in turn are influenced by the theological doctrines in which they are trained in their church. But the attitude of priests towards theological doctrines may also be affected by the resistances they encounter in the attitudes toward worship among their flocks. Of course, not all believers (or priests) will react in the same way, and thus arise the possibilities of schism and heresy.[212]

This describes the fact that worship practices are not dependent on *a priori* doctrines, which are grasped by means of reason in an unmediated fashion. In other words, it rejects the notion that you first hold a belief and then subsequently turn to various practices. However, the theology of glory endorses the notion that we must reason beyond the earth, spiritually connect with God, and then subsequently engage practices. As noted above, Vanhoozer does put forward the text as primary in contrast to pure speculation, but he still wrongly regards practices as secondary. Was there no religion or beliefs until the Bible appeared? Surely, practices and traditions are what we subsequently find in the text. The practices and language we use form the beliefs we hold and show what we believe.

From a Wittgensteinian view, it is important to turn to the maxim of Prosper of Aquitaine, 'The law of worshiping founds the law of believing', in contrast to the theology of glory's inversion, 'The law of believing founds the law of worship.' Belief is necessarily tied to practice as Wittgenstein writes,

> The stream of life, or the stream of the world, flows on and our propositions are so to speak verified at instants.

> Our propositions are only verified by the present. And
> so in some way they must be commensurable with the
> present; and they cannot be so in spite of their spatio-
> temporal nature; on the contrary this must be related
> to their commensurability as the corporeality of a ruler
> is to its being extended – which is what enables it to
> measure.[213]

Theology is understood as tied to contextual markers (rules);
namely, practices. This is not in spite of their 'spatio-temporal
nature', it is because of it. Once again, this does not mean that
there is a reduction to the worshipping community, as Fergus
Kerr rightly notes,

> we are always already related in a variety of
> commonalities that constitute our life together – but the
> temptation to a placid immersion in the communal is as
> destructive to humanity as illusory aspirations of escaping
> it. It is a denial of our humanity to aspire to the condition
> of the wordless self, but it is just as much a denial of our
> humanity not to have such aspirations.[214]

To lose theological meaning is to lose the associated practices
(measurement), not the transcendent referent.

Given the importance of not separating theology and practice, it should be clear that the history of practice, that is, tradition, is likewise significant. Rhees says,

> Within a single tradition, like that of the Hebrew
> religion, it can be said that the author of the second
> half of Isaiah meant the same by 'God' as the author
> (or authors) of Genesis did, and that St. Paul meant the
> same by 'God' as both of them because of the continuity
> of Hebrew worship and the kind of worship that was,
> the importance of such conceptions as 'the God of our
> fathers', 'the God of Abraham and the God of Jacob', and
> so on. But for Paul the same God could be worshipped
> by gentiles who were not the seed of Abraham and Jacob.
> And if gentiles worship the same God, then this must

appear in what they say about God, in the way they
worship and in what it means to them to be creatures and
children of God. To ask '*Do* they worship the same God
or not?' is to ask about that.[215]

The significance of tradition is not that it is an epistemological
relation, nor is it a private determination; rather, it is that which
is the given and open to view, it is before our eyes, it is our
practices. Does this make the tradition arbitrary? Wittgenstein
says, 'tradition is not something a man can learn; not a thread
he can pick up when he feels like it; any more than a man can
choose his own ancestors. Someone lacking a tradition who
would like to have one is like a man unhappily in love.'[216]
Just as Wittgenstein points out the significance of language-
games as connected to all that surrounds them, so tradition
is connected to all that surrounds it – neither are private or
arbitrary. Paul Holmer also sees the tradition of language and
theology as a significant basis of meaning and practices, 'for
just as grammar of a language is not quite an invention, nor do
we simply make up our logical rules, so we do not design theology just to suit ourselves,' rather, 'the grammar of a language
is that set of rules that describes how people speak what are
doing it well and with efficacy.'[217] Consequently, believing is
not the individual activity of determining which propositions
correlate with transcendent truths; rather, as Wittgenstein says,
'Believing means submitting to authority.'[218] The authority
submitted to is not that of reason, metaphysics, or epistemology, it is that of tradition. In a sense, we submit to the authority
of tradition passively, just as we submit to the human history
of language passively.

What does this mean for dialogue from a Wittgensteinian perspective? It should be clear that he would not be interested in any
theory that supposedly makes dialogue easier, but only succeeds
in blurring and confusing real differences. Therefore, the question is not which is the right theory, or even which theory is best.
Instead, Wittgenstein would look at practices. When we leave
the rough ground anything can be said, which amounts to nothing being said. Rhees writes, 'If someone said that *all* that matters
is purity of heart, or the pure love of God, and that traditional

forms of worship and prayer don't matter – then the phrase "pure love of God" may become as empty as any "dead" ceremony is.'[219] In which case Wittgenstein's remark is well suited, 'We have got on to slippery ice where there is no friction and so in a certain sense the conditions are ideal, but also, just because of that, we are unable to walk. We want to walk: so we need *friction*. Back to the rough ground!'[220] Practices hit the rough ground and continue the tradition, and it is this aspect of theology that speaks and engages dialogue.

This is why ecumenical discussions that seek unity behind or between practices are misguided. Ecumenical thought seems to hold the opinion that various denominations may hold various doctrines and practices, but that which is between or underneath the doctrines and practices will eventually, through dialogue, be recognized as the mutual truth – therefore, we can have ecumenical success, we are in agreement! The problem is that the truth is not under or between practices and doctrines; instead, it is in the practices and doctrines. Granted, if you want ecumenical success then abstractions will get you there much quicker. However, to reach this conclusion, you must first separate practice and worship from theology. The doctrines are not irrelevant, and neither are the practices to which they are tied. Instead, what are not relevant are theories and new words about unknown things between doctrines, between theories and between doctrines and theories. These empty spaces are what Wittgenstein would call instances of 'language idling' and 'on holiday'. What were always important for Wittgenstein were differences in practice, not unity in abstraction. He says, 'my interest is in showing that things which look the same are really different. I was thinking of using as a motto for my book a quotation from *King Lear*: "I'll teach you differences"'.[221] The problem is not that there are different practices and doctrines; it is that there are theories about spaces between or beyond these differences, and that with the right theory about these empty spaces we can all agree – on what?

What does this mean for ecumenical progress? The desire for ecumenical success, however good-intentioned, is in line with the theology of glory. Wittgenstein notes, concerning progress in philosophy, that it 'satisfies a longing for the transcendent, because in so far as people think they can see the "limits of human understanding", they believe of course that they can see beyond these'.[222] This also applies to theology when we think we can see beyond the limits and beyond the practices and doctrines; however, those are the only things we can see.

Chapter 8

Explanations, Doubt and Redemption

My intent in the preceding was to show that Wittgenstein's philosophy is analogical to a religious point of view, and in particular to Chalcedonian Christology. To prove or disprove that Wittgenstein was religious, or even that he literally has a religious point of view, would be overly ambitious – perhaps impossible. Yet to add depth to the discussion it is worthwhile to address specific remarks Wittgenstein makes concerning Christianity, as well as to look briefly at what others have ventured in this respect.

Norman Malcolm's well-known work, *Wittgenstein: A Religious Point of View?* also addresses Wittgenstein's philosophy in analogical terms. He provides an illuminating discussion of Wittgenstein's philosophy, yet he does not engage any one particular religious viewpoint. He notes:

> Wittgenstein did much religious thinking: but religious thoughts do not figure in his detailed treatments of the philosophical problems. It would seem, therefore, that when he spoke of seeing those problems 'from a religious point of view', he did not mean that he conceived of them as religious problems, but instead that there was similarity, or similarities, between his conception of philosophy and something that is characteristic of religious thinking.[223]

More specifically, Malcolm centres on 'Wittgenstein's conception of the grammar of language, and his view of what is paramount in religious life.

> First, in both there is an end to explanation; second, in both there is an inclination to be amazed at the existence

of something: third, into both there enters the notion of an 'illness'; forth, in both, *doing, acting*, takes priority over the intellectual understanding and reasoning.[224]

Malcolm rightly looks for the analogical rather than equivocal relation between Wittgenstein's philosophy and a religious point of view.

We have already seen that there is a limit to explanation largely within Wittgenstein's later thought, and it is this aspect that Malcolm emphasizes, 'It is pointless to continue seeking for an explanation. We are faced with a fact which we must *accept*. "That's how it is!" The words, "It is God's will", have many religious connotations: but they also have a logical force similar to "That's how it is!" Both expressions tell us to stop asking "Why" and instead *accept a fact!*'[225] It follows that 'the word "explanation" appears in many different language-games, and is used differently in different games . . . An explanation is *internal* to a particular language-game. There is no explanation that *rises above* our langue-games, and explains *them*. This would be a *super-concept* of explanation – which means that it is an ill conceived fantasy.'[226] The notion that we can rise above the language-games is comparable to the theology of glory seeking knowledge beyond our everyday practice and lives and instead searching for the justification or explanation of religious belief. As Wittgenstein observes, there is a temptation to excessive explanations, we want a place from which to stand with our reason and say we fully understand, and if we apply this to theology, we are tempted to be more than human – we want to be like God to have 'super-knowledge'.

The analogical amazement that Malcolm mentions is found in the fact that the language-games cannot be explained. Wittgenstein says, 'Let yourself be struck by the existence of the language-games.'[227] Moreover, since the language-games are not explained from a realm outside of the language-games, and are not understood simply through ratiocination, it follows that Malcolm's analogy of the priority of doing and acting is well-founded. Wittgenstein himself notes that 'it is our *acting*, which lies at the bottom of the language game.'[228]

The analogical element of illness is then turning to excessive rationalization. Wittgenstein says, 'Our illness is this, to want to explain.'[229] Moreover, 'The philosopher's treatment of a question is like the treatment of an illness.'[230] The philosopher treats illness by removing or at least showing the problem of excessive explanation. Consequently, as Wittgenstein notes, 'all that philosophy can do is destroy idols'; and importantly, 'that means not creating a new one'.[231]

The point of removing the problematic explanations and theories is not to provide better explanations and theories. Wittgenstein says, 'A philosopher is a man who has to cure many intellectual diseases in himself before he can arrive at the notions of common sense.'[232] However, he notes

> a remarkable and characteristic phenomena in
> philosophical investigation: the difficulty – I might
> say – is not that of finding the solution but rather of
> recognising as the solution something that looks as if
> it were only a preliminary to it . . . This is connected,
> I believe, with our wrongly expecting an explanation,
> whereas the solution of the difficulty is a description,
> if we give it the right place in our considerations. If
> we dwell upon it, and do not try to get beyond it. The
> difficulty here is: to stop.[233]

Common sense knows when to stop.

Does the fact that Wittgenstein's philosophy seeks to put a stop to excessive explanatory effort show that his philosophy is analogical to a religious point of view? Malcolm provides a useful overview of Wittgenstein's philosophy, but as Peter Winch rightly sees, he does not provide a clear example of an analogical religious point of view. However, Winch thinks that he has evidence of a religious point of view in a letter that Wittgenstein wrote to Drury, who was disheartened with his career:

> Don't think about yourself, but think of others . . . You
> said in the park yesterday that possibly you had made a
> mistake in taking up medicine: you immediately added
> that probably it was wrong to think such a thing at all. I

117

am sure it is. But not because being a doctor you may not go the wrong way, or go to the dogs, but because if you do, this has nothing to do with the choice of profession being a mistake. For what human being can say what would have been the right thing if this is the wrong one? You didn't make a mistake because there was nothing at the time you knew or ought to have known that you overlooked. Only this one could have called making a mistake: and even if you had made a mistake in this sense, this would now have to be regarded as a datum as all other circumstances inside and outside which you can't alter (control). The thing now is to live in the world in which you are, not to think or dream about the world you would like to be in. Look at people's sufferings, physical and mental, you have them close at hand, and this ought to be a good remedy for your troubles. Another way is to take a rest whenever you ought to take one and collect yourself . . . As to religious thoughts I do not think the craving for placidity is religious: I think a religious person regards placidity or peace as a gift from heaven, not something one ought to hunt after. Look at your patients more closely as human beings in trouble and enjoy the opportunity you have to say 'good night' to so many people. This alone is a gift from heaven which many people would envy you. And this sort of thing ought to heal your frayed soul, I believe. I think in some sense you don't look at people's faces closely enough.[234]

In light of this letter, Winch concludes that Wittgenstein is concerned with Drury's 'spiritual welfare' and that it 'clearly expresses the quasi-religious idea that life imposes certain duties on us' and the letter accomplishes this through a philosophical point.[235] Nonetheless, Winch concludes, as does Malcolm, that they do not have a definitive answer to Wittgenstein's religious point of view. Winch notes, 'I am grateful to Norman Malcolm, as for so much else, for making me think about the whole issue in a way I should probably not otherwise have come to. Of course he himself explicitly disclaimed any pretension to finality or certainly in his interpretation. And I want to make the same sort of disclaimer.'[236] But it is not necessary for either Malcolm or Winch to make such a disclaimer. Why make a disclaimer when nothing firm is provided anyway. Despite providing a good discussion of Wittgenstein's thought, they never clearly or concretely discuss a religious point of view. Indeed, their discussions of Wittgenstein's religious point of view are vague, or as Winch himself says, 'very sketchy'.[237]

Whereas neither Malcolm nor Winch venture any firm interpretation, John Canfield and Brian Clack do take an interpretive stance on Wittgenstein's religious point of view. Canfield, purporting to be working in an analogical framework, concludes, 'Wittgenstein's later philosophy and doctrines of Mahayana Buddhism integral to Zen coincide in a fundamental aspect; for Wittgenstein language has, one might say, a mystical base; and this base is exactly the Buddhist ideal of acting with a mind empty of thought.'[238] While Clack states, 'Our question . . . is whether atheism is the inevitable consequence of an acceptance of Wittgenstein's approach to religious belief, and what kind of atheism that could be' his answer is a

> despairing, apocalyptic atheism that arises from
> Wittgenstein's philosophy of religion, the frustrated and
> bitter recognition that the passionate beauty of the religious
> life is no longer open to us. Moreover, it would . . . be
> somewhat perplexing were someone to accept all that
> Wittgenstein has to say about religion in his later period
> and yet still be able to continue in his or her faith.[239]

Not only do Canfield and Clack provide theories that, from my perspective, are entirely misplaced, they also provide them with certainty.

In contrast to Malcolm and Winch my intent was to show a clear and concrete theological point of view, and in contrast to Canfield and Clack, I claim no finality or certainty for the analogical relation. Analogies are always somewhat ill fitting, so the question is how tolerable they are. I do not think Zen Buddhism is tolerable as 'fundamental' and 'exact', and it is intolerable to imagine that the best analogy or equivalence for Wittgenstein's thought is a 'despairing, apocalyptic atheism'. I think that it is best to let Wittgenstein speak for himself, and he never discusses Zen Buddhism or an 'apocalyptic atheism', but he does discuss Christianity in insightful ways.

I have argued previously in *Wittgenstein's Religious Point of View* that Wittgenstein's philosophy is analogical to a Hebraic point of view.[240] This present study carries the Hebraic view further into Christian thought on the basis of the shift from the Old to the New – from the Old Testament to the New Testament, and from Wittgenstein's self described old thoughts to the new ones. This transition represents continuity and distinction in terms of God and logic moving from the hidden to the revealed in the New Testament and *On Certainty* respectively. Now it is possible to add character to this theological point of view by discussing several of Wittgenstein's remarks on Christianity. Once again, I am not in any manner trying to imply, prove or disprove that Wittgenstein was a Christian by means of these remarks; rather, they provide an interesting point of view.

Wittgenstein's rejection of excessive explanation in a Christian context can be seen in his letter to Drury, who was thinking of becoming a priest:

> Just imagine trying to preach a sermon every Sunday:
> you couldn't do it, you couldn't possibly do it. I would be
> afraid that you would try and elaborate a philosophical
> interpretation or defence of the Christian religion. The
> symbolism of Christianity is wonderful beyond words,
> but when people try to make a philosophical system out
> of it I find it disgusting.[241]

Indeed, Wittgenstein says, 'If Christianity is the truth, then all the philosophy about it is false.'[242] The theologian teaches practices and the grammar of faith, not the justification of, or theory about, faith. Needless to say, this is contrary to approaches such as Swinburne's use of Bayes' theorem to conclude in his work *The Resurrection of God Incarnate* that the resurrection has a 97 per cent probability of occurring.[243] I would like to see the reaction of a congregation where the minister, impressed with this scholarly theory, informs them that the resurrection has a 3 per cent chance of never occurring – be assured that your faith is probably correct.

In opposition to such theories, Wittgenstein noted, 'If you can accept the miracle that God became man, then all these difficulties are as nothing . . .' and Drury responded: 'One of the early Church Fathers, Lactantius I think, said something like that. Novels and plays must indeed be probable, but why should this, the scheme of man's redemption, be probable? Wittgenstein: I am glad to hear that I had the same thought as one of the Church Fathers.'[244] Moreover, Drury notes:

> I mentioned to Wittgenstein that I was reading
> Dr Tennant's book entitled Philosophical Theology,
> which had just been published. Wittgenstein: A title like
> that sounds to me as if it would be something indecent.
> Drury: Tennant tries to revive in a complicated way
> the 'argument from design'. Wittgenstein: You know
> I am not one to praise this present age, but that does
> sound to me as being 'old-fashioned' in a bad sense.
> Drury: Tennnant is found of repeating Butler's aphorism,
> 'Probability is the guide of life'. Wittgenstein: Can you
> imagine St Augustine saying that the existence of God
> was 'highly probable'![245]

Once probabilities are mentioned it is clear that someone did not know when to stop. Wittgenstein rightly observes,

> We are misled by this way of putting it: 'This is a good
> ground, for it makes the occurrence of the event probable.'
> That is as if we had asserted something further about the
> ground, which justified it as a ground; whereas to say that
> this ground makes the occurrence probable is to say nothing
> except that this ground comes up to a particular standard of
> good grounds – but the standard has no grounds![246]

All of the explanations and resultant probabilities devalue the Christian faith.

Wittgenstein notes that it is more profound, in contrast to Schlick, to say the good is good because God wants it, rather than God wants the good because it is good, 'For it cuts off the way to any explanation "why" it is good, while the second is the shallow, rationalistic one, which proceeds "as if" you could give reasons for what is good.'[247] Likewise, why is there value in Beethoven? Because of the rhythm? Perhaps the notes? Wittgenstein says, 'whatever I was told, I would reject, and that not because the explanation was false but because it was an explanation.'[248] If someone gave an explanation for Christianity, then that explanation should also be rejected on the grounds that it is an explanation, not because it is a good or bad explanation. Indeed, Wittgenstein says, 'Anyone who reads the Epistles will find it said: not only that it is not reasonable, but that it is folly. Not only is it not reasonable, but it doesn't pretend to be. What seems to me ludicrous about O'Hara is his making it appear to be *reasonable*.'[249]

The theologians of glory fall under Wittgenstein's criticism of Father O'Hara for trying to defend Christian belief by making it into a sort of science. They both constantly see the method of science before their eyes, and are irresistibly tempted to ask and to answer questions in the way science does, and 'this tendency is the real source of metaphysics and leads philosophers [and theologians] into complete darkness.'[250] Wittgenstein had nothing against science, only the idea that science provides the only avenue to knowledge, that there is a strict separation in all things between what is measurable and objective and what is not, and that this represents the limit of meaning – including theological meaning.

From a Wittgensteinian view, explanations do not give value or justification to Christianity; instead, they fail to recognize the nature Christianity and actually devalue it. Ray Monk notes this in Wittgenstein's remark to Drury:

'Russell and the parsons between them have done infinite harm, infinite harm.' Why pair Russell and the parsons in one condemnation? Because both have encouraged the idea that philosophical justification for religious beliefs is necessary for those beliefs to be given any credence. Both the atheist, who scorns religion because he has found no evidence for its tenants, and the believer, who attempts to prove the existence of God, have fallen victim to the 'other' – to the idol-worship of the scientific style of thinking.[251]

For Wittgenstein, the division is not between those who believe and those who do not. The division rests on the distinction between those who seek the best explanation for the evidence in contrast to those who do not. Theological language is clearly not an interpretation of the world, nor is it an explanation of the world (as if it is an epistemological issue); rather, it is an issue in logic – how the world is for the religious believer. Theology is not simply offering a different explanation from that of the atheist; instead, it is a different world, one with a spiritual reality. Thus, rejecting theology and God is not an empirical conclusion; it is an *a priori* rejection of the spiritual.

Not only are explanations and justifications problematic, so are the various theories within theology that attempt to provide the best viewpoint. Holmer rightly sees this problem:

> In such places, the sheer opulence of points of view
> and the thick harvest of historical antecedents give a
> revivification by scholarship and cause dim overviews
> to develop about the development of doctrine and the
> necessity that one succeed another. After a while, it
> becomes a lot easier to believe this vague metaview that
> makes one skeptical about any particular theology of an
> individual or of a church than it is to be a lively believer
> and hearty participant in any one theology and its related
> practices. The point that seems so disturbing here is that
> these chaotic developmental views are so easy to teach
> and that they are no longer linked up with anything save
> the most obvious accommodation to the 'Zeitgeist'. They
> serve also to divorce most people from the practice of
> religion itself, and instead create a sophisticated clientele
> that is interested in theology as one more artifact cast up
> in the course of time.[252]

Consequently, theology is often 'lumped with the special interests, and, by its detractors, finally, with astrology, prescientific thought, mythology, and make-believe'.[253] When theology is placed in an apologetic role or in a progression of theoretical models, it succumbs to these categories and is rightly rejected as unreasonable and as out of fashion.

The continual building of explanatory theories relates well to Kierkegaard's thoughts:

> Most systematizers in relation to their systems are like a man who builds an enormous castle and himself lives alongside it in a shed; they themselves do not live in the enormous systematic building. But in the realm of mind and spirit this nonresidence is and remains a decisive objection. Spiritually understood, a man's thoughts must be the building in which he lives – otherwise the whole thing is deranged.[254]

The castle is like the theories in the theology of glory, it gives the appearance of something grand, but is actually a nonresidence, that is, it is entirely detached from the world, life and practices. But for that very reason it is ideal in contrast to the fleeting world. However, if people say that theology has no meaning for them, then a definition or theory is not what is being asked for, it is no help to invite them into your imaginary castle. Such questions require direction to the use of words and the form of life through real interconnections.

An example of turning away from the rough world to the ideal is seen in one of Wittgenstein's favourite books. Once again, Wittgenstein took a copy of *The Brothers Karamazov* to the Russian front and memorized much of it. It is natural to wonder what aspect of this book caught his attention. Perhaps it is the contrast between Ivan and Father Zosima. In the text Ivan represents the theology of glory – thinking takes precedence over looking. Ivan is more interested in Euclidean ideas than in what is open to view; namely, humanity.[255] As the early Wittgenstein devalues the clothes of language in favour of the invisible simple object to determine meaning, so Ivan devalues the human world in favour of what he sees as a meaningful calculus. He says, 'one can love one's neighbour in the abstract, and sometimes even at a distance, but at close quarters it is almost impossible.'[256] The rough nature of humanity makes it impossible to deal with and he would rather think in the world of pure thought. Ferapont also rejects the rough nature of the world and renounces Zosima's life since he 'was seduced by sweets . . . he sipped tea, he worshipped his belly, filing it with sweet things and his mind with haughty thought . . . and for this he is put to shame'.[257] The flight to the castles that reason builds and away from the world is reminiscent of Socrates' response to Simmias in the *Phaedo*, 'Do you think it is part of a philosopher to be concerned with such so-called pleasures as those of food and drink?' and Simmias's response, 'I think the true philosopher despises them.'[258] Likewise, Rhees says,

> Plato takes the question about life to be one about the *intelligibility* of life. It is in that sense that he places the emphasis which he does upon the unity of life, which he connects with the Parmenidean unity of being, or unity of discourse. I think this is important in lots of ways, but I might note at the start how far this is from the Hebrew and Christian concern with life: how far it is from the idea of making one's life a sacrifice.[259]

Both Ivan and Ferapont reject the world and the life of Zosima and continue the theology of glory's separation of the divine and the human, the world and reason.

Dostoevsky shows that this separation between the physical and the spiritual is too great, and on this point is similar to Wittgenstein. The important point is not unity with a transcendent realm (Ivan and Ferapont); it is living in the shed of the rough world (Zosima, Alesha) and making one's life a sacrifice. The world and our bodies are not that which distract us or deter us from a spiritual reality, they are the means of the spiritual reality. Likewise, Wittgenstein observes, 'the human body is the best picture of the human soul',[260] and 'the face is the soul of the body'.[261]

The continual desire to separate the human from the divine, and to place priority on reason, is found through the history of Christianity, but it has been rejected at various times and in various ways. The early abstract search for God beyond Jesus was answered by Gregory of Nyssa who says there is no experience beyond Jesus, the ethical path was answered by Augustine who notes that we are turned inwards and have no good in ourselves, and the path of knowledge through philosophy was answered by Luther who noted that true theology is at the cross. Wittgenstein is not a theologian and does not focus on Christianity, but his philosophy is useful in a similar manner. Recall that he says if there were a place that he could reach only by means of a ladder he would not; likewise, the above theologians throw away the ladders of moralism and rationalism. Moreover, Wittgenstein regards thought and language as coextensive,[262] that is, the mind is fixed to the rough ground, not abstractions and rationalizations. Likewise, Luther regards paradise, from which humans were ejected, to be a place where they had a better understanding of their creaturehood, not where they had divine wisdom and knowledge. This then leads to humbleness, the mind cannot take flight to a metaphysical castle, we cannot take flight to God with our morals or reason.

This humbleness is evident in Wittgenstein's favourite story by Tolstoy; namely, *Three Hermits*. Wittgenstein notes, 'My favorite is the story of the three hermits who could only pray, "You are three we are three have mercy upon us".'[263] In this story a bishop on his sailing route sees a small island and his curiosity leads him to investigate, whereupon he meets three old hermits:

I wished to see you, servants of God, and to do what I can to teach you, also. The old men looked at each other smiling, but remained silent. 'Tell me,' said the Bishop, 'what you are doing to save your souls, and how you serve God on this island.' The second hermit sighed, and looked at the oldest, the very ancient one. The latter smiled, and said: 'We do not know how to serve God. We only serve and support ourselves, servant of God.' 'But how do you pray to God?' asked the Bishop. 'We pray in this way,' replied the hermit. 'Three are ye, three are we, have mercy upon us.' And when the old man said this, all three raised their eyes to heaven, and repeated: 'Three are ye, three are we, have mercy upon us!' The Bishop smiled. 'You have evidently heard something about the Holy Trinity,' said he. 'But you do not pray aright.'[264]

So the Bishop proceeds to teach them the Lord's Payer, and subsequently sails away; however, he suddenly notices something following them.

Look there, what is that, my friend? 'What is it?' the Bishop repeated, though he could now see plainly what it was – the three hermits running upon the water, all gleaming white, their grey beards shining, and approaching the ship as quickly as though it were not morning. The steersman looked and let go the helm in terror. 'Oh Lord! The hermits are running after us on the water as though it were dry land!' The passengers hearing him, jumped up, and crowded to the stern. They saw the hermits coming along hand in hand, and the two outer ones beckoning the ship to stop. All three were gliding along upon the water without moving their feet. Before the ship could be stopped, the hermits had reached it, and raising their heads, all three as with one voice, began to say: 'We have forgotten your teaching, servant of God. As long as we kept repeating it we remembered, but when we stopped saying it for a time, a word dropped out, and now it has all gone to pieces. We can remember nothing of it. Teach us again.' The Bishop crossed himself, and leaning over the ship's side, said: 'Your own prayer will reach the Lord, men of God. It is not for me to teach you. Pray for us sinners.'[265]

The humble nature of the hermits and their hope for mercy is essential – not their status or great learning.

Not only were the hermits contrasted with the Bishop, they can also be contrasted with a street preacher Wittgenstein came across. Drury notes,

we passed a street preacher who was proclaiming in a loud, raucous voice all that Jesus Christ had done for him.

127

Wittgenstein shook his head sadly [and remarked] . . . If he really meant what he was shouting, he wouldn't be speaking in that tone of voice. This is a kind of vulgarity in which at least you can be sure that the Roman Catholic Church will never indulge.[266]

It is difficult to know exactly what Wittgenstein was thinking, but it is possible that he considered the street preacher to be shouting words that had no relationship to those passing by, and simply by adding more force to his exclamations he did not add any more force to his point. Likewise, it is not the case that apologetics will convince others of the truth of Christianity, as if the stronger the argument the more convincing it is.

Theology is not a matter of convincing people by means of explanations and theories. If the point is not explanations and theories to convince people, then what can remove their doubts? Wittgenstein says, 'What combats doubt is, as it were, *redemption*. Holding fast to this must be holding fast to belief.'[267] Wittgenstein notes that the Christian religion is not for those who want the best explanation for the world (in an empirical sense); rather, he says,

The Christian religion is only for the man who needs infinite help, solely, that is, for the man who experiences infinite torment. . . . Anyone in such torment who has the gift of opening his heart, rather than contracting it, accepts the means of salvation in his heart. Someone who in this way penitently opens his heart to God in confession lays it open for other men too. In doing this he loses the dignity that goes with his personal prestige and becomes like a child. That means without official position, dignity or disparity from others. A man can bare himself before others only out of a particular kind of love. A love which acknowledges, as it were, that we are all wicked children.[268]

Shortly before his death, he wrote, 'God may say to me: "I am judging you out of your own mouth. Your own actions have made you shudder with disgust when you have seen other people do them".'[269] Consequently, it seems that Wittgenstein included himself along with those who despair, and with those who do not need intellectual proof, but mercy. He says, 'People are religious to the extent that they believe themselves to be not so much *imperfect*, as ill. Any man who is half-way decent will think himself extremely imperfect, but a religious man thinks himself *wretched*.'[270] Once again, explanations cannot address 'infinite torment' or 'consciousness of sin'. What can address these religious issues is, as Wittgenstein says, redemption.

The theology of glory offers a Christian philosophy that competes with various world views, while the theology of the cross is not a philosophy or system, it does not place the individual as an observer of principles which can then be judged; rather, it is the individual who is judged – and perhaps redeemed. Wittgenstein notes:

> Life can educate one to a belief in God. And experiences too are what bring this about; but I don't mean visions and other forms of sense experience which show us the 'existence of this being', but, e.g., sufferings of various sorts. These neither show us God in the way a sense impression shows us an object, nor do they give rise to conjectures about him.[271]

Instead, this suffering and despair shows the need of a merciful God. Thus, Wittgenstein observes,

> if I am to be REALLY saved, – what I need is certainty – not wisdom, dreams or speculation – and this certainty is faith. And faith is faith in what is needed by my heart, my soul, not my speculative intelligence. For it is my soul with its passions, as it were with its flesh and blood, that has to be saved, not my abstract mind.[272]

D. H. Lawrence also observes this blood knowing in contrast to rationalism, he notes:

> My great religion is a belief in the blood, the flesh, as being wiser than the intellect. We can go wrong in our

minds. But what our blood feels and believes and says, is always true. The intellect is only a bit and bridle. What do I care about knowledge. All I want is to answer to my blood, direct, without fribbling intervention of mind, moral, or what not. I conceive a man's body as a kind of flame, like a candle flame forever upright yet flowing: and the intellect is just the light that is shed onto the things around . . . We have got so ridiculously mindful, that we never know that we ourselves are anything – we think there are only objects we shine on. . . .[273]

Doubt is not resolved with further theories and explanations; rather, doubt is dissolved with redemption in terms of the flesh and blood.

Interestingly, Wittgenstein writes:

What inclines even me to believe in Christ's Resurrection? It is as though I play with the thought – If he did not rise from the dead, then he is decomposed in the grave like any other man. *He is dead and decomposed.* In that case he is a teacher like any other and can no longer *help*; and once more we are orphaned and alone. So we have to content ourselves with wisdom and speculation. We are in a sort of hell where we can do nothing but dream, roofed in, as it were, and cut off from heaven.[274]

On the one hand, there is the perspective that the separation between humans and the divine is one of a strict division whereby the two cannot meet, as is found in the Nestorian perspective. This is similar to Wittgenstein's criticism of overlooking practices in the rough world, as if they are dead. Yet by means of reason there may be glimpses of the transcendent and divine that could convince us of the likelihood of a God, as is found in the theology of glory. The problem, however, is that this sets up ladders of reason, morals, status, etc., that can lead to pride in one's imaginary castle. This is the viewpoint that actually cuts us off from heaven.

On the other hand, if the separation is not simply between the human and the divine, but is between sin and the divine, then everything changes. To focus on the former leads some to think that reason can address the problem as if it is a matter of castle building; however, the latter is addressed, as Wittgenstein says, through redemption. This is the perspective of the theology of the cross, seeing the divine through suffering, and in that suffering seeing the substantial union of humans with the divine in accord with Chalcedonian Christology. The context shifts from the transcendent to the rough world, where God is revealed in a manger and at the cross – not a castle. Consequently, the ladders lead nowhere but to the pride of imaginary climbing. This is in accord with Wittgenstein's philosophy seeing meaning in practices, not speculations that transcend our language or a logical syntax underneath our language. Likewise, Paul says to the Romans that Christ is not in Heaven to be called down, nor is he in the deep to be called up, but is contemporarily the Word in your heart and mouth.[275] Consequently, as Wittgenstein notes, 'Christianity is not a doctrine, not, I mean, a theory about what has happened and will happen to the human soul, but a description of something that actually takes place in human life. For "consciousness of sin" is a real event and so are despair and salvation through faith.'[276] Redemption becomes more significant than explanations, and consciousness of sin becomes more significant than an awareness of non-omniscience. From this viewpoint, we are no longer 'roofed in' and 'cut off from heaven', not because we can escape our shed and secure connections to external strictures or collapse the distinctions, but because – as Wittgenstein says he is inclined to believe as necessary – Christ comes to our shed, is human and divine, and is risen.

Notes

1. M. O'C. Drury, 'Conversations with Wittgenstein', in *Recollections of Wittgenstein,* ed. Rush Rhees (Oxford: Oxford University Press, 1984), 79.
2. Brian R. Clack, *An Introduction to Wittgenstein's Philosophy of Religion* (Edinburgh: Edinburgh University Press, 1999).
3. Phillip R. Shields, *Logic and Sin in the Writings of Ludwig Wittgenstein* (Chicago: University of Chicago Press, 1993).
4. Ludwig Wittgenstein, *Culture and Value,* ed. G. H. von Wright in collaboration with Heikki Nyman, trans. Peter Winch (Chicago: University of Chicago Press, 1984), 17e.
5. Ludwig Wittgenstein, *Philosophical Investigations*, trans. G. E. M. Anscombe (Oxford: Basil Blackwell, 1988), §118.
6. Ludwig Wittgenstein, *Remarks on Frazer's Golden Bough*, ed. Rush Rhees, trans. A. C. Miles, revised by Rush Rhees (Atlantic Highlands: Humanities Press International, 1978), 1e.
7. Wittgenstein, *Culture and Value*, 34e.
8. Wittgenstein, *Philosophical Investigations*, § 309.
9. Drury, 'Conversations with Wittgenstein', 143.
10. Ibid., 114.
11. Wittgenstein, *Culture and Value*, 35e.
12. Wittgenstein, *Philosophical Investigations*, viii.
13. Ibid., § 107.
14. Wittgenstein, *Culture and Value*, 33e.
15. Ibid., 57e.
16. Drury, 'Conversations with Wittgenstein', 120.
17. Wittgenstein quoted in Ray Monk, *Ludwig Wittgenstein: The Duty of Genius* (London: Jonathan Cape, 1990), 496.
18. M. O'C. Drury, 'Some Notes on Conversations', in *Recollections of Wittgenstein,* ed. Rush Rhees (Oxford: Oxford University Press, 1984), 77.
19. Bertrand Russell, *Principles of Mathematics,* (Cambridge: University Press, 1903), 528.
20. Bertrand Russell, 'Obituary: Ludwig Wittgenstein', *Mind*, 60, 1951, 297–98.
21. Wittgenstein, quoted in Monk, *Ludwig Wittgenstein: The Duty of Genius* (London: Jonathan Cape, 1990), 106.
22. Rush Rhees, 'Postscript', in *Recollections of Wittgenstein,* ed. Rush Rhees (Oxford: Oxford University Press, 1984), 214.

23. Dury, 'Conversations with Wittgenstein', 114.
24. Rush Rhees, 'Postscript', 215.
25. Drury, 'Conversations with Wittgenstein', 112.
26. Monk, 353.
27. Drury, 'Conversations with Wittgenstein', 141.
28. Nicolas Badusen, *Lectures and Essays*, 1963.
29. Wittgenstein, quoted in Monk, 459.
30. Ibid., 493.
31. Ibid., 498.
32. Wittgenstein, *Culture and Value*, 66e.
33. Wittgenstein, quoted in Monk, 558.
34. Drury, 'Conversations with Wittgenstein', 148.
35. Ibid., 168.
36. *The Philosophical Writings of Descartes*, trans. J. Cottingham, R. Stoothoff and D. Murdoch (Cambridge: Cambridge University Press, 1985), 1:114–115.
37. Ibid., 2:12.
38. Ibid., 2:15.
39. Ibid., 2:17.
40. Ibid., 1:126–27.
41. Ibid., 2:49.
42. Ibid., 2:35.
43. Ibid., 1:14.
44. Ibid., 1:127.
45. Ibid., 3:190.
46. Ibid., 3:336.
47. Rebecca D. Pentz, 'Veatch and Brain Death: A Plea for the Soul', *The Journal of Clinical Ethics*, 5, 2 (Summer 1994), 132.
48. *The Philosophical Writings of Descartes*, 2:56.
49. John Locke, *An Essay concerning Human Understanding*, ed. with a Foreword by Peter H. Nidditch (Oxford: Clarendon Press, 1985), 43.
50. John Locke, *The Works of John Locke in Nine Volumes*, vol. 3 (London: Rivington, 1824), Chapter: 'A Letter To The Right Reverend Edward, Lord Bishop Of Worchester, concerning Some Passages relating to Mr. Locke's Essay Of Human Understanding', 1–96.
51. Locke, *An Essay concerning Human Understanding*, 48.
52. Ibid., 104.
53. Ibid.
54. Ibid., 563.
55. Ibid., 406–07.
56. Ludwig Wittgenstein, *Tractatus Logico-Philosophicus*, trans. C. K. Ogden, with an Introduction by Bertrand Russell (London: Routledge & Kegan Paul, 1986), 4.016.
57. Wittgenstein, *Tractatus Logico-Philosophicus*, 4.01.
58. Ibid., 3.22.
59. Ludwig Wittgenstein, *Notebooks*, ed. G. H. von Wright and G. E. M. Anscombe, trans. G. E. M. Anscombe (Oxford: Blackwell, 1979), 62.

60. Wittgenstein, *Tractatus Logico-Philosophicus*, 1.1–1.12.

61. Ibid., 4.26.

62. Ibid., 4.001.

63. Ibid., 7.

64. Paul Engelmann, *Letters from Ludwig Wittgenstein, with a Memoir*, ed. B. F. McGuinness, trans. L. Furtmüller (Oxford: Basil Blackwell, 1967), 97.

65. Wittgenstein, *Tractatus Logico-Philosophicus*, 5.55.

66. Ibid., 4.002.

67. George Berkeley, *A Treatise concerning the Principles of Human Knowledge*, ed. with an Introduction by G. J. Warnock (La Salle, IL: Open Court, 1962), § 15.

68. George Berkeley, *Siris: A Chain of Philosophical Reflexions and Inquiries concerning the Virtues of Tar Water*, (London, 1747), § 302.

69. Wittgenstein, *Tractatus Logico-Philosophicus*, 6.53.

70. Wittgenstein, *Philosophical Investigations*, § 309.

71. Ibid., viii.

72. Wittgenstein, *Culture and Value*, 63e.

73. Wittgenstein, *On Certainty*, 467.

74. Ibid., 58.

75. Wittgenstein, *Tractatus Logico-Philosophicus*, 6.51.

76. Wittgenstein, *Philosophical Investigations*, § 136.

77. Wittgenstein, *Philosophical Grammar*, ed. Rush Rhees, trans. A. C. Miles, revised by Rush Rhees (Atlantic Highlands: Humanities Press International, 1989), 211.

78. Ibid., 121.

79. Wittgenstein, *Philosophical Investigations*, § 19.

80. Ibid., 1.

81. Ibid.

82. Augustine, *Confessions*, bk I, ch. 8. Wittgenstein, *Philosophical Investigations*, § 1.

83. Wittgenstein, *Philosophical Investigations*, § 1.

84. Ibid., § 27.

85. Ibid., § 32.

86. Noam Chomsky, *Aspects of the Theory of Syntax* (Cambridge, MA: M.I.T. Press, 1965), 25.

87. Jerry Fodor. *The Language of Thought* (Hassocks, Sussex: Harvester Press, 1975), 64.

88. Wittgenstein, *Philosophical Investigations*, § 43.

89. Ibid., § 380.

90. Ibid.

91. Ibid., § 381.

92. Wittgenstein, *On Certainty*, 61.

93. Wittgenstein, *Philosophical Investigations*, § 23.

94. Ludwig Wittgenstein, *Remarks on the Foundations of Mathematics*, ed. G. H. von Wright, Rush Rhees and G. E. M. Anscombe, trans. G. E. M. Anscombe (Oxford: Basil Blackwell, 1978), 5.

95. Wittgenstein, *Philosophical Grammar*, 185.

Notes

96. Wittgenstein, *Culture and Value*, 30e.

97. Wittgenstein, *Philosophical Investigations*, § 116.

98. Ibid., § 126.

99. Ibid., § 67

100. Ibid., § 18.

101. Bernard Williams, 'Wittgenstein and Idealism', in *Understanding Wittgenstein*, Royal Institute of Philosophy Lectures, ed. Godfrey Vesey, vol. 7 (London: Macmillan, 1972–73), 95.

102. Wittgenstein, *Philosophical Investigations*, § 415.

103. Ibid., § 241.

104. Wittgenstein, *Remarks on the Foundations of Mathematics*, iv.

105. Wittgenstein, *On Certainty*, 109–110.

106. Ibid., 204.

107. Ibid., 476.

108. Ludwig Wittgenstein, *The Blue and Brown Books* (Oxford: Basil Blackwell, 1972), 24.

109. Wittgenstein, *On Certainty*, 143–44.

110. Ibid., 559.

111. Ibid., 477.

112. Ibid., 94.

113. Ibid., 248.

114. Ludwig Wittgenstein, 'Sections 86–93 (pp. 405–35) of the so-called "Big Typescript",' ed. Heikki Nyman, trans. C. G. Luckhardt and M. A. E. Aue, *Synthese*, 87, 1 (April, 1991), 6.

115. Wittgenstein, *On Certainty*, 51.

116. Ibid., 105.

117. Drury, 'Conversations with Wittgenstein', 161.

118. Wittgenstein, *Philosophical Investigations*, § 107.

119. Wittgenstein, *Culture and Value*, 7e.

120. Tertullian, *The Prescription Against Heretics* (Whitefish, MT: Kessinger Publishing, 2004), 12–13.

121. Kai Nielsen, 'Wittgensteinian Fideism', *Philosophy*, 42, 161 (1967), 191–209, 192.

122. Wittgenstein, *Philosophical Investigations*, § 66.

123. Wittgenstein, *Culture and Value*, 72e.

124. Paul Holmer, *The Grammar of Faith* (San Francisco: Harper & Row, 1978), 184.

125. Holmer, 184.

126. Norman Geisler (ed.), *Biblical Errancy: An Analysis of its Philosophical Roots*. (Grand Rapids: Zondervan Publishing House, 1981), 201.

127. Plato, *Phaedo*, trans. G. M. A. Grube (Indianapolis: Hackett Publishing, 1977), 66a.

128. Wittgenstein, *Philosophical Investigations*, § 245.

129. Ibid., § 256.

130. Thomas Hobbes, 'Third Set of Objections with the Author's Replies', 'First Objection' in *The Philosophical Writings of Descartes*, 2:121.

131. Solomon Schechter, *Aspects of Rabbinic Theology*, with an introduction by Neil Gillman and by Louis Finkelstein (Woodstock,VT: Jewish Lights Publishing, 1993), 22.

132. Abraham Heschel, *The Prophets* (New York: Harper & Row, 1962), 275.

133. John Calvin, *John Calvin: Institutes of the Christian Religion*, trans. Henry Beveridge (London: Arnold Hatfield, 1599) bk 1, ch. 15, sec. 2.

134. Ibid., bk 1, ch. 15, sec. 2.

135. Ibid., bk.1, ch. 3, sec. 1.

136. Friedrich Nietzsche, *Twilight of the Idols*, trans. R. J. Hollingdale (Harmondsworth: Penguin, 1968), 106.

137. Ludwig Wittgenstein, *Philosophical Remarks*, ed. Rush Rhees, trans. Raymond Hargreaves and Roger White (Oxford: Basil Blackwell, 1975), Foreword.

138. Wittgenstein, *Remarks on the Foundations of Mathematics*, 333.

139. Wittgenstein, *Philosophical Grammar*, 193.

140. Nestorius, *The Bazaar of Heraleides*, trans. G. R. Driver and Leonard Hodgson (Oxford: Clarendon Press, 1925), 27.

141. Theodore of Mopsuestia, *ad Baptizandos*, quoted in R. V. Sellars, *The Council of Chalcedon: A Historical and Doctrinal Survey* (London: S. P. C. K., 1961), 162.

142. Eranistes, quoted in, Harry Wolfson, *The Philosophy of the Church Fathers*, vol. I (Cambridge, MA: Harvard University Press, 1964), 445.

143. *Enchiridion Symbolorum*, ed. Henricus Denzinger (Barcelona: Herder, 1963), 108.

144. Martin Luther, *Luther's Works: American Edition*, vol.37, ed. Jaroslav Pelikan and Helmut T. Lehmann (St. Loius: Concordia Publishing House; Minneapolis: Augsburg Fotress Press, 1955–86), 37:210–11.

145. Zwingli, 'Exposition of the Faith', in *The Library of Christian Classics*, vol. 24, *Zwingli and Bullinger* (Philadelphia: The Westminster Press, 1953), 252.

146. Martin Luther, quoted in *The Two Natures in Christ*, by Martin Chemnitz (St. Louis: Concordia Publishing House, 1971), 191–92.

147. Wittgenstein, *Culture and Value*, 35e.

148. Isaiah 55.8.

149. Wittgenstein, *Philosophical Investigations*, viii.

150. Wittgenstein, 'Sections 86–93 (pp. 405–35) of the so-called "Big Typescript"', 9.

151. Wittgenstein, *Philosophical Investigations*, § 66.

152. Shields, 33.

153. Locke, *An Essay concerning Human Understanding*, 697.

154. Ibid., 89.

155. Bertrand Russell, *Why I am not a Christian* (New York: Simon & Simon, 1957), 3.

156. Alvin Plantinga, 'Reason and Belief in God', in *Faith and Rationality: Reason and Belief in God*, ed. Alvin Plantiga and Nicholas Wolterstorff (Notre Dame, 1983), 60.

157. Calvin, bk 1, ch. 3, sec. 1.

Notes

158. Nicholas Wolterstorff, 'Reformed Epistemology' in *Philosophy of Religion in the 21st Century*, ed. D. Z. Phillips and Timothy Tessin (Basingstoke: Palgrave, 2001), 50.

159. *The Philosophical Writings of Descartes*, 1:18.

160. Heschel, *Between God and Man: An Interpretation of Judaism* (New York: Harper Brothers, 1959), 108.

161. Wittgenstein, *Philosophical Investigations*, § 38.

162. George A. Lindbeck, *The Nature of Doctrine: Religion and Theology in a Post-liberal Age*. (Philadelphia: The Westminster Press), 16.

163. Ibid., 32.

164. Ibid., 17.

165. Ibid., 18.

166. Ibid., 118.

167. Ibid., 83.

168. Ibid., 18.

169. Ibid., 64.

170. Ibid., 69.

171. Drury, 'Conversations with Wittgenstein', 157.

172. Kevin Vanhoozer, *First Theology: God, Scriptures & Hermeneutics.* (Downers Grove, IL: InterVarsity Press, 2002), 222.

173. Kevin Vanhoozer, *The Drama of Doctrine: A Canonical-linguistic Approach to Christian Theology* (Louisville, KY: Westminster John Knox Press, 2005), 172.

174. Ibid., 96.

175. Ibid., 97.

176. Ibid., 11.

177. Ibid., 294.

178. Ibid., 117–18.

179. Ibid., 304.

180. Friedrich Nietzsche, *Beyond Good and Evil*, trans. Helen Zimmern and Walter Kaufmann (New York: Vintage Books, 1966), part I, 22.

181. Wittgenstein, *Philosophical Investigations*, § 107.

182. Martin Luther, 'Heidelberg Disputation', in *Martin Luther's Basic Theological Writings*, ed. Timothy F. Lull with a Foreword by Jarsolav Pelikan (Minneapolis: Fortress Press, 1989), 43.

183. Tertullian, *The Prescription Against Heretics* (Whitefish, MT: Kessinger Publishing, 2004), 12–13.

184. Wittgenstein, *Culture and Value*, 50e.

185. Drury, 'Conversations with Wittgenstein', 115.

186. Rush Rhees, *Rush Rhees on Religion and Philosophy*, ed. D. Z. Phillps and Mario von der Ruhr (Cambridge: Cambridge University Press, 1997), 181.

187. Lindbeck, *The Nature of Doctrine*, 66.

188. Wittgenstein, *Culture and Value*, 80e.

189. Wittgenstein, *Philosophical Investigations*, § 116.

190. Wittgenstein, *Culture and Value*, 7e.

Notes

191. Dietrich Bonhoeffer, *Letter and Papers from Prison* (London: SCM Press, 1971), 376.

192. Luther, quoted in *The Present Day Christological Debate,* by Klass Runia (Downers Grove, IL: InterVarsity Press, 1984), 97.

193. Luther, *Luther's Works*, 8:27.

194. Wittgenstein, *On Certainty*, 51.

195. Ludwig Wittgenstein, *Wittgenstein's Lectures: 1932–1935, from the notes of Alice Ambrose and Margrete MacDonald, ed. Alice Ambrose* (Chicago: University of Chicago Press, 1989), 32.

196. Luther, *Luther's Works*, 2:15.

197. Drury, 'Conversations with Wittgenstein', 164–65.

198. Wittgenstein, *Culture and Value*, 32e.

199. Martin Luther, *D. Martin Luthers Werke; kritische Gesamtausgabe.* (Weimar: H. Bohlau, 1883), 17:183:37.

200. Wittgenstein, *Culture and Value*, 32e.

201. Ulrich Zwingli, 'On True and False Religion', in *The Latin Works of Ulrich Zwingli*, ed. S. M. Jackson, vol. 3 (Philadelphia: Heidelberg Press, 1912–29), 211, 214.

202. Luther, *Luther's Works*, 37:72.

203. Wittgenstein, *On Certainty*, 501.

204. Rhees, *Rush Rhees on Religion and Philosophy*, 199.

205. Calvin, bk 1, ch. 3, sec. 3.

206. Rhees, *Rush Rhees on Religion and Philosophy*, 181.

207. Luther, *Luther's Works*, 52:39–40.

208. Rhees, *Rush Rhees on Religion and Philosophy*, 61.

209. Fergus Kerr, *Theology After Wittgenstein* (Oxford: Basil Blackwell, 1997), 158.

210. Rhees, *Rush Rhees on Religion and Philosophy*, 45.

211. Ibid., 44.

212. Peter Winch, 'Meaning and Religious Language', in *Reason and Religion*, ed. Brown S. (Ithaca, NY: Cornell University Press, 1977), 202.

213. Wittgenstein, *Philosophical Remarks*, 81.

214. Kerr, 212.

215. Rhees, *Rush Rhees on Religion and Philosophy*, 46–7.

216. Wittgenstein, *Culture and Value*, 76e.

217. Holmer, 20.

218. Wittgenstein, *Culture and Value*, 45e.

219. Rhees, *Rush Rhees on Religion and Philosophy*, 116.

220. Wittgenstein, *Philosophical Investigations*, § 107.

221. Drury, 'Conversations with Wittgenstein', 157.

222. Wittgenstein, *Culture and Value*, 15e.

223. Norman Malcolm, *Wittgenstein: A Religious Point of View?*, ed. Peter Winch (New York: Cornell University Press, 1995), 24.

224. Ibid., 92.

225. Ibid., 86.

226. Ibid., 77–8.

227. Wittgenstein, *Philosophical Investigations*, p. 224.

Notes

228. Wittgenstein, *On Certainty*, 204.

229. Wittgenstein, *Remarks on the Foundations of Mathematics*, 333.

230. Wittgenstein, *Philosophical Investigations*, § 255.

231. Wittgenstein, 'Sections 86–93 (pp. 405–35) of the so-called "Big Type-script",' 9.

232. Wittgenstein, *Culture and Value*, 44e.

233. Ludwig Wittgenstein, *Zettel*, ed. G. E. M. Anscombe and G. H. von Wright, trans. G. E. M. Anscombe (Oxford: Blackwell, 1967), 314.

234. Drury, 'Conversations with Wittgenstein', 95.

235. Peter Winch, 'Discussion of Malcolm's Essay', in *Wittgenstein: A Religious Point of View?*, ed. P. Winch (New York: Cornell University), 126.

236. Ibid.

237. Ibid., 124.

238. John V. Canfield, 'Wittgenstein and Zen', *Philosophy*, 50, 194 (October 1975), 383.

239. Brian R. Clack, *An Introduction to Wittgenstein's Philosophy of Religion* (Edinburgh: Edinburgh University Press, 1999), 125, 129.

240. Tim Labron, *Wittgenstein's Religious Point of View* (London; New York: Continuum, 2006).

241. Drury, 'Conversations with Wittgenstein', 86.

242. Wittgenstein, *Culture and Value*, 83e.

243. Richard Swinburne, *The Resurrection of God Incarnate* (Oxford: Oxford University Press, 2003), 214.

244. Drury, 'Conversations with Wittgenstein', 164–65.

245. Drury, 'Some Notes on Conversations', 90.

246. Wittgenstein, *Philosophical Investigations*, § 482.

247. Ludwig Wittgenstein, quoted in *Wittgenstein and the Vienna Circle*, Conversations recorded by Freidrich Waismann, trans. Joachim Schulte and Brian McGuiness (Oxford: Basil Blackwell, 1979), 115.

248. Ibid., 116.

249. Ludwig Wittgenstein, *Lectures and Conversations on Aesthetics, Psychology and Religious Belief*, ed. Cyril Barret (Berkeley: University of California Press), 58.

250. Wittgenstein, *The Blue and Brown Books* (Oxford: Basil Blackwell, 1958), 18.

251. Wittgenstein quoted in Monk, 410.

252. Holmer, 3.

253. Ibid., 1.

254. *Soren Kierkegaard's Journals and Papers*, ed. and trans. by Howard V. Hong and Edna H. Hong assisted by Gregor Malantschuk, vol. 3, 1846 (Bloomington and London: Indiana University Press, 1975), 519.

255. Fyodor Dostoevsky, *The Brothers Karamazov* (New York: W. W. Norton, 1976), 179.

256. Ibid., 184.

257. Ibid., 312–314.

258. Plato, *Phaedo*, 64d–e.

259. Rhees, *Rush Rhees on Religions and Philosophy*, 179.

260. Wittgenstein, *Philosophical Investigations*, p. 178.
261. Wittgenstein, *Culture and Value*, 23e.
262. Wittgenstein, *Philosophical Investigations*, § 329.
263. Drury, 'Some Notes on Conversations', 86.
264. Tolstoy, 'Three Hermits', in *Twenty-three Tales*, trans. L and A. Maude, Funk and Wagnall Company New York, 1907, scanned by Harry Plantinga, 1995 (Christian Classics Ethereal Library), 14.
265. Ibid.
266. Drury, 'Conversations with Wittgenstein', 111.
267. Wittgenstein, *Culture and Value*, 33e.
268. Ibid., 46.
269. Ibid., 87.
270. Ibid., 45.
271. Ibid., 86.
272. Ibid., 33.
273. D. H. Lawrence, *The Letters of D. H. Lawrence*, ed. J. T. Boulton, vol. 1 (Cambridge: Cambridge University Press, 1979), 503.
274. Wittgenstein, *Culture and Value*, 33e.
275. Romans 10.6–8.
276. Wittgenstein, *Culture and Value*, 28e.

Bibliography

Augustine, Saint. *Confessions*. Translated by R. S. Pine-Coffin. London: Penguin Books, 1961.

Berkeley, George. *A Treatise concerning the Principles of Human Knowledge*. Edited with an Introduction by G. J. Warnock. La Salle, IL: Open Court, 1962.

— *Siris: A Chain of Philosophical Reflexions and Inquiries concerning the Virtues of Tar Water*. London, 1747.

Bernard, Williams. 'Wittgenstein and Idealism', in *Understanding Wittgenstein*, Royal Institute of Philosophy Lectures, Vol. 7. Edited by Godfrey Vesey, 76–95. London: Macmillan, 1972–73.

Bonhoeffer, Dietrich. *Letters and Papers From Prison*. London: SCM Press, 1971.

Calvin, John. *John Calvin: Institutes of the Christian Religion*. Translated by Henry Beveridge. London: Arnold Hatfield, 1599.

Canfield, John V. 'Wittgenstein and Zen'. *Philosophy*, 50, 194 (October 1975), 383–408.

Chemnitz, Martin. *The Two Natures in Christ*. St. Louis: Concordia Publishing House, 1971.

Chomsky, Noam. *Aspects of the Theory of Syntax*. Cambridge, MA: M.I.T. Press, 1965.

Clack, Brian R. *An Introduction to Wittgenstein's Philosophy of Religion*. Edinburgh: Edinburgh University Press, 1999.

Descartes, Rene. *The Philosophical Writings of Descartes*. Translated by John Cottingham, Robert Stoothoff, Dugald Mudoch. 2 volumes. Cambridge: Cambridge University Press, 1985.

— *The Philosophical Writings of Descartes*. Translated by John Cottingham, Robert Stoothoff, Dugald Murdoch, Anthony Kenny. Vol. 3, *The Correspondence*. Cambridge: Cambridge University Press, 1991.

Doestoevsky, Fyodor. *The Brothers Karamazov*. Translated by Ralph E. Matlan. New York: W. W. Norton, 1976.

Drury, M. O'C. 'Conversations with Wittgenstein', in *Recollections of Wittgenstein*. Edited by Rush Rhees, 97–171. Oxford: Oxford University Press, 1984

— 'Some Notes on Conversations with Wittgenstein', in *Recollections of Wittgenstein*. Edited by Rush Rhees, 76–96. Oxford: Oxford University Press, 1984.

Bibliography

Engelmann, Paul. *Letters From Ludwig Wittgenstein, with a Memoir.* Edited by B. F. McGuinness. Translated by L. Furtmüller. Oxford: Basil Blackwell, 1967.

Eranistes. In *The Philosophy of The Church Fathers.* By Harry Wolfson. Vol. 1. Cambridge, MA: Harvard University Press, 1964.

Fodor, Jerry. *The Language of Thought.* Hassocks, Sussex: Harvester Press, 1975.

Heschel, Abraham Joshua. *Between God and Man: An Interpretation of Judaism.* New York: Harper Brothers, 1959.

— *The Prophets.* New York: Harper and Row, 1962.

Hobbes, Thomas. 'Third Set of Objections with the Author's Replies', in *The Philosophical Writings of Descartes,* 2:121. Translated by John Cottingham, Robert Stoothoff, Dugald Mudoch. Cambridge: Cambridge University Press, 1985.

Holmer, Paul. *The Grammar of Faith.* San Francisco: Harper & Row, 1978.

Geisler, Norman. Editor. *Biblical Errancy: An Analysis of its Philosophical Roots.* Grand Rapids: Zondervan Publishing House, 1981.

Kerr, Fergus. *Theology after Wittgenstein.* Oxford: Basil Blackwell, 1986.

Kierkegaard, Soren. *Soren Kierkegaard's Journals and Papers.* Edited and translated by Howard V. Hong and Edna H. Hong assisted by Gregor Malantschuk. Vol. 3. Bloomington and London: Indiana University Press, 1975.

Labron, Tim. *Wittgenstein's Religious Point of View.* New York; London: Continuum, 2006.

Lawrence, D. H. *The Letters of D. H. Lawrence.* Edited by J. T. Boulton. Vol. 1. Cambridge: Cambridge University Press, 1979.

Lindbeck, George. *The Nature of Doctrine: Religion and Theology in a Postliberal Age.* Philadelphia: The Westminster Press, 1984.

Locke, John. *An Essay Concerning Human Understanding.* Edited with a Foreword by Peter H. Nidditch. Oxford: Clarendon Press, 1985.

Luther, Martin. *Luther's Works: American Edition.* 55 volumes. Edited by Jaroslav Pelikan and Helmut T. Lehmann. St. Louis: Concordia Publishing House; Minneapolis: Augsburg Fortress Press, 1955–1986.

— *D. Martin Luthers Werke; kritische Gesamtausgabe.* Weimar: H. Böhlau, 1883, 17:183:37.

— *Martin Luther's Basic Theological Writings.* Edited by Timothy F. Lull with a Foreword by Jaroslav Pelikan. Minneapolis: Fortress Press, 1989.

— In Klass Runia, *The Present Day Christological Debate.* Downers Grove, IL: InterVarsity Press, 1984.

Malcolm, Norman. *Wittgenstein: A Religious Point of View?* Edited by Peter Winch. New York: Cornell University Press, 1995.

Monk, Ray. *Ludwig Wittgenstein: The Duty of Genius.* London: Jonathan Cape, 1990.

Nestorius. *The Bazaar of Heraleides.* Translated by G. R. Driver and Leonard Hodgson. Oxford: Clarendon Press, 1925.

Nielsen, Kai. 'Wittgensteinian Fideism'. *Philosophy,* 42, 161 (1967), 191–209.

Nietzsche, Friedrich. *Beyond Good and Evil.* Translated by Helen Zimmern and Walter Kaufmann. New York: Vintage Books, 1966.

Bibliography

— *Twilight of the Idols*. Translated by R. J. Hollingdale. Harmondsworth: Penguin, 1968.

Pentz, Rebecca D. 'Veatch and Brain Death: A Plea for the Soul'. *The Journal of Clinical Ethics*, 5, 2 (Summer 1994), 132–35.

Plantinga, Alvin. 'Reason and Belief in God', in *Faith and Rationality: Reason and Belief in God*. Edited by Alvin Plantinga and Nicholas, 16–93. Woltersorff: Notre dame, 1983.

Plato. *Phaedo*. Translated by G. M. A. Grube. Indianapolis: Hackett Publishing, 1977.

Russell, Bertrand. 'Obituary: Ludwig Wittgenstein'. *Mind,* 60 (1951), 297–98.

— *Principles of Mathematics*. Cambridge: Cambridge University Press, 1903.

— *Why I am Not a Christian*. New York: Simon & Simon, 1957.

Schechter, Solomon. *Aspects of Rabbinic Theology*, with introductions by Neil Gillman and Louis Finkelstein. Woodstock, VT: Jewish Lights Publishing, 1993.

Sellars, R. V. *The Council of Chalcedon: A Historical and Doctrinal Survey*. London: S. P. C. K, 1961.

Shields, Philip R. *Logic and Sin in the Writings of Ludwig Wittgenstein*. London: University of Chicago Press, 1993.

Swinburne, Richard. *The Resurrection of God Incarnate*. Oxford: Oxford University Press, 2003.

Tertullian. *The Prescription Against Heretics*. Whitefish, MT: Kessinger Publishing, 2004.

Tolstoy. *Twenty-three Tales*. Translated by L. and A. Maude. New York: Funk and Wagnall Company, 1907.

Vanhoozer, Kevin. *First Theology: God, Scriptures & Hermeneutics*. Downers Grove, IL: InterVarsity Press, 2002.

— *The Drama of Doctrine: A Canonical-Linguistic Approach to Christian Theology*. Louisville, KY: Westminster John Knox Press, 2005.

Winch, Peter. 'Discussion of Malcolm's Essay', in *Wittgenstein: A Religious Point of View?* Edited by Peter Winch, 95–135. New York: Cornell University Press, 1995.

— 'Meaning and Religious Language', in *Reason and Religion*. Edited by S. Brown, 193–221. Ithaca, New York: Cornell University Press, 1977.

Wittgenstein, Ludwig. *Culture and Value*. Edited by G. H. von Wright in collaboration with Heikki Nyman. Translated by Peter Winch. Chicago: The University of Chicago Press, 1984.

— *Wittgenstein's Lectures, 1930–32. From the Notes of John King and Desmond Lee*. Edited by Desmond Lee. Chicago: The University of Chicago Press, 1989.

— *Wittgenstein's Lectures, 1932–35. From the Notes of Alice Ambrose and Margaret MacDonald*. Edited by Alice Ambrose. Chicago: The University of Chicago Press, 1989.

— *Lectures and Conversations on Aesthetics, Psychology and Religious Belief.* Edited by Cyril Barret. Berkeley: University of California Press, 1966.

Bibliography

Wittgenstein, Ludwig. *Notebooks*. Edited by G. H. von Wright and G. E. M. Anscombe. Translated by G. E. M. Anscombe. Oxford: Blackwell, 1979.

— *On Certainty*. Edited by G. E. M. Anscombe and G. H. von Wright. Translated by Denis Paul and G. E. M. Anscombe. Oxford: Basil Blackwell, 1979.

— *Philosophical Grammar*. Edited by Rush Rhees. Translated by A. J. P. Kenny. Oxford: Blackwell, 1974.

— *Philosophical Investigations*. Translated by G. E. M. Anscombe. Oxford: Basil Blackwell, 1988.

— *Philosophical Remarks*. Edited by Rush Rhees. Translated by Raymond Hargreaves and Roger White. Oxford: Basil Blackwell, 1975.

— *Remarks on Frazer's Golden Bough*. Edited by Rush Rhees. Translated by A. C. Miles, revised by Rush Rhees. Atlantic Highlands: Humanities Press International, 1989.

— *Remarks on the Foundations of Mathematics*. Edited by G. H. von Wright, Rush Rhees, G. E. M. Anscombe. Translated by G. E. M. Anscombe. Oxford: Basil Blackwell, 1978.

— 'Sections 86–93 (pp. 405–35) of the so-called "Big Typescript"'. Edited by Heikki Nyman. Translated by C. G. Luckhardt and M. A. E. Aue. *Synthese*, 87, 1 (April, 1991): 3–22.

— *The Blue and Brown Books*. Oxford: Basil Blackwell, 1972.

— *Tractatus Logico-Philosophicus*. Translated by C. K. Ogden. London: Routledge & Kegan Paul, 1986.

— *Zettel*. Edited by G. E. M. Anscombe and G. H. von Wright. Translated by G. E. M. Anscombe. Oxford: Blackwell, 1967.

— *Wittgenstein and the Vienna Circle*. Conversations recorded by Friedrich Waismann. Edited by Brian McGuinness. Translated by Joachim Schulte and Brain McGuinness. Oxford: Basil Blackwell, 1979.

Wolterstorff, Nicholas. 'Reformed Epistemology', in *Philosophy of Religion in the 21st Century*. Edited by D. Z. Phillips and Timothy Tessin, 39–63. Basingstoke: Palgrave, 2001.

Zwingli, Ulrich. 'Exposition of the Faith', in *The Library of Christian Classics*. Vol. 24, *Zwingli and Bullinger*, 245–79. Philadelphia: The Westminster Press, 1953.

— *Commentary on True and False Religion*, Edited by Samuel Macauley Jackson and Clarence Nevin Heller, Durham, North Carolina: Labyrinth Press, 1981.

Index

Index

Index

Index

Index

Index